circ', 3
LAD: 3/2008

How Bill James Changed Our View of Baseball

by Colleagues, Critics, Competitors and Just Plain Fans

How Bill James Changed Our View of Baseball

by Colleagues, Critics, Competitors and Just Plain Fans

edited by Gregory F. Augustine Pierce

How Bill James Changed Our View of Baseball
by Colleagues, Critics, Competitors and Just Plain Fans
edited by Gregory F. Augustine Pierce

Cover Photo by Jean Clough
Cover design by Tom A. Wright
Text design and typesetting by Patricia A. Lynch

Published by ACTA Sports, a division of ACTA Publications, 5559 W. Howard Street, Skokie, IL 60077 (800) 397-2282 www.actasports.com

Library of Congress Number: 2006940210
ISBN 10: 0-87946-317-1
ISBN 13: 978-0-87946-317-5
Printed in Canada
Year: 15 14 13 12 11 10 9 8 7
Printing: 10 9 8 7 6 5 4 3 2 1

Contents

**Dedicated to the Ken Phelpses
of the World**

Introduction

by Gregory F. Augustine Pierce

President of ACTA Publications
and editor of *Diamond Presence*

I've loved baseball since I was a young boy, but I never heard of Bill James until I discovered a hardcover edition of *The New Bill James Historical Baseball Abstract* in a bookstore in 2001 and said to my wife, "I know what I want for Christmas."

A couple months later, John Dewan came to me with an offer I couldn't refuse: He would buy into my little religious publishing house and we would open up a second line of books we would call ACTA Sports. Oh, and by the way, John was a good friend of Bill James. My parents didn't raise a dummy, so I agreed to the deal, and as a bonus I got to meet Bill James. As many of the writers in this book point out, that is an interesting experience, because James is not necessarily what you'd expect.

First of all, he loves baseball more than he likes statistics. He told me he started all his statistical analysis so he could understand the game better. Besides, he said, he likes to give his opinion whenever possible and he found that doing the statistical analysis helped him back up his opinions with more than just feeling, instinct, or even casual observation.

Second, he is a very generous guy. Generous with his opinions, certainly, but also generous with his knowledge. From what I can tell, James really believes that information about baseball (and I assume other things in life) is meant to be shared. He does this, I think, not only because he wants others to enjoy baseball as much as he does but also because he genuinely wants his analysis and theories to be tested and refined by others. In this he is a true scientist.

Even more, as these essays also show, James is generous with others, especially younger or non-professional baseball people who want to learn to think like he thinks. There are many stories in these pages about how his generosity led to someone's career or discovery of self.

Still, I must admit that I was surprised and even a little skeptical when *Time* magazine named Bill James one of the "100 Most Influential People in the World" in April of 2006. James was included on a list with world political, religious, business, educational, art and entertainment leaders. Give me a break, I thought. He's an interesting person, but one of the hundred most influential people in the WORLD? Up there with people looking for a cure for cancer or ways to bring about world peace?

So I started asking people why Bill James would ever be included on a list like that, and I began to get some interesting answers. It turns out that what he is doing with baseball has all kinds of applications in other walks of life. It is not just that he has changed how people think about baseball; he has changed how a whole generation of people think about a lot of things.

I asked twelve people who know James' work well to describe how he had influenced them and others, and this book is the result. In it you will find full essays by professional sports writers such as Alan Schwarz and Sam Walker; protégés of Bill James such as John Dewan, Daryl Morey, Steve Moyer, Rob Neyer and Dave Studenmund; colleagues, competitors or observers of James such as Gary Huckabay, Hal Richman, Ron Shandler and John Thorn; and, with a truly unique take on the subject, James' wife Susan McCarthy.

You will also find shorter comments by others, some well-known and most "just plain fans," all of whom wanted to weigh in. They include doctors, lawyers, engineers, college professors and students, baseball announcers and bloggers, writers (technical and not), a software architect, consultants of various kinds, and even some retired Wall Street executives and military personnel.

Finally, I offered Bill James the opportunity to have "The Last Word" after the book was written, and (to my surprise) he agreed. That doesn't mean he read the entire manuscript. Maybe he did; maybe he didn't. But he certainly knew what we were up to, and he responded in the same spirit.

So I think I was wrong. Bill James does belong on a list of influential people, even though his area of expertise is baseball analysis. He must. The people in this book say so, and so might you after you read it.

Freeing My Mind

by Alan Schwarz

senior writer for *Baseball America*
and author of *The Numbers Game* and *Once Upon a Game*

This is not what my father had in mind.

When Dad flew my brother and me to London and Paris in the spring of 1983, he surely had visions of teenaged Ken and Alan encountering such history, such majesty, such…well, enlightenment. Castles. Cathedrals. I could pick up a few books—Voltaire, some Pepys perhaps.

But instead of William the Conqueror, I read about Willie Wilson. At the Louvre, the only LeMaster I learned about was Johnny. Al Oliver toppled Oliver Cromwell. This will no doubt mortify my old man, from whom I kept my increasingly rumpled *1983 Bill James Baseball Abstract* stealthily stashed in my backpack and who to this day believes that my nose was buried in matter considerably more worldly during that fortnight. But I can come clean now, Dad. After all, in some ways, this is when I became me.

***

Bruce Springsteen had a wonderful line many years ago about Bob Dylan: "Dylan freed your mind the way Elvis freed your body." Well, throughout that Europe trip and for the next several years, Bill James freed my mind. I can identify many influences up and down

Before I read my first *Baseball Abstract* in the 1970s, I absorbed much of my baseball knowledge from newspapers, magazines, TV and radio announcers, *Sporting News* reporters, and baseball book authors. For me, James has successfully shown most of them to be wrong most of the time. Because of him, I enjoy the world's best game with an almost spiritual glee. BOOYAH!

MIKE FLEMING
Writer
Tallahassee, Florida

my time line, people who taught me how to think: Bugs Bunny, F. Scott Fitzgerald, Phil Ochs. (OK, mostly Bugs Bunny.) But in terms of one single person who gave me a rhetorical road map, all but implanted an intellectual compass between my temples, it was Bill James.

I loved baseball, of course. Topps baseball cards, Phil Rizzuto doing Yankee games, the whole bit. And I loved mathematics, ever since my father taught me square roots when I was four. But Bill James meant more to me than a mix of baseball and numbers. First was his sharp skepticism of baseball's conventional wisdom, his unrelenting demand: 'Is this true? Or have boneheads duped us into thinking it is?' (Yes, open contempt ranked behind only Twinkies and naps on the list of this teenager's delights.) But what gave Bill James such traction was the words. James' use of language around the numbers was so dazzling, its levers and mass as aesthetically and purposefully balanced as a pendulum clock, that even a fourteen-year-old could tell he was reading baseball's Galileo. The Ptolemaists were in deep trouble.

About those words. The guy was downright hilarious. "Did you ever notice that players named White are almost always black, and players named Black are usually white?" read James' comment on Frank White in the *1983 Abstract*. "The Royals also had a Black on their roster, Bud, who of course is white; in fact, the Royals had to set some sort of record by having four colored people on their team, White, Black, Blue and Brown. Scott Brown is not any browner than anybody else, Vida is definitely not Blue, nor for that matter is Darryl Motley."

And as an outsider, with no deference to relationships within the game, James wrote with shocking spasms of candor. Poor Enos Cabell, he wailed, "can't play first, can't play third, can't hit, can't run and can't throw. So who cares what his attitude is?" When Reggie Jackson babbled on about how Eddie Murray possessed the "character" and "fortitude" to break out of a slump, James wrote, "Many athletes truly believe that they are successful at what they do not because God made them strong and fast and agile, but because *they're better people than the rest of us.... That's* where all the bullshit about clutch ability comes from."

The Baseball Abstract, at its heart, was wildly entertaining—intelligent, amusing, and a Christmas tree of numbers, each page a new ornament that refracted light in different directions. James didn't use those statistics to win trivia contests but to understand the game's inner workings better and to beseech others to heed their call. He would hear some announcer prattle on about how baseball is seventy-five percent pitching and then go and try to figure out if that made any sense. (It didn't.) When a manager claimed that players reach their primes at ages thirty-one and thirty-two, he checked the records to see if they were right. (They weren't.)

And God help Rickey Henderson fans. Pages 176 and 177 of my first *Abstract* in 1983 are what hooked me forever. In less than three columns of numbers and stiletto paragraphs, James sliced up Henderson's 130 stolen bases the previous season—a total that left most fans and writers slapping their foreheads in amazement—into a pile of overrated mush. Keep in mind that in 1983 almost no one, particularly this high school freshman from suburban New York, had heard of Pete Palmer's Linear Weights or understood the true cost of a caught stealing. This was the age of Omar Moreno. Miguel Dilone. Stolen bases were *good*, period.

Well, maybe not. James explained to us—systematically breaking down how many runs Henderson created and how many he would have created had he just plopped himself crosslegged on first—that the difference was maybe about 11. And then…what about the 42 caught stealings? Those 42 extra outs revised the estimate of runs Henderson created to about 4.5. "Four and a half goddamn runs, and they want to give him an MVP award for it," James wrote in a stirring crescendo. "Rickey Henderson's stolen base attempts didn't mean anything to the Oakland A's—nothing at all. He's a great young ballplayer, but his selfish pursuit of the stolen-base record did not help the Oakland A's. It hurt them." The baseball establishment thought this wacky Kansan was high as a kite. But whatever James was smoking, I puffed away gladly.

***

Bill James didn't invent statistical baseball analysis—F.C. Lane did shockingly advanced work in the first decades of the twentieth century, while George Lindsey, Earnshaw Cook, Eric Walker and others had already performed historic number-crunching without the fanfare. But more than anyone, James popularized statistical analysis and made it a legitimate phenomenon, particularly by indoctrinating young people like me. Every year he gave us new widgets to play with: understanding how ballparks distorted hitters like Carney Lansford and Jose Cruz; seeing teams through the Plexiglas

Principle; Brock2 career projections; and the aptly-named Favorite Toy, which estimated players' chances of reaching 3,000 hits and 500 home runs. (Man, Jason Thompson tailed off, huh?) From Similarity Scores to Major League Equivalencies, from Pitcher Run Support to Leadoff Efficiency, Bill James laid out laws for our wonderful game that just…made sense, all fitting together in a magnificent, interlocking Tinkertoy. In the end, the twelve annual *Abstracts* that Bill James published from 1977 through 1988 stand today as baseball's version of Euclid's *Elements,* a textbook series for generations to come.

I was in the first generation. I wound up majoring in mathematics in college and planned to become a high school math teacher, but through Bill James—as well as through John Allen Paulos' *Innu-*

When I was a teenager, I loved baseball and started dabbling in analysis of its numbers—even searching for information on platoon splits at the library at Cooperstown on a summer trip with my family. For me, reading my first *Abstract* in the spring of 1984, and particularly its introductory essays "Inside-Out Perspective" and "Logic and Methods in Baseball Analysis," was validation that there was an expanded way to view the game. From that point forward, my view of the game changed to one where the primary question I asked myself was not "what happened?" but "why did it happen?" That mindset, based on logical reasoning and inculcated by reading Bill James, has served me well in areas that transcend baseball.

DAN FOX
Software Architect
Colorado Springs, Colorado

meracy, a delightful little book— I saw that writing and mathematics were actually quite compatible. (Both disciplines dab from similar palettes, applying logic and proportion and metaphor to get its audience from A to B.) In my desperate quest to avoid neckties, I decided to give sports writing a whirl, got hired by *Baseball America*, and in the subsequent sixteen years since—in *B.A.*, *The New York Times* and way too many other publications—have written more than two million words on baseball. I don't bow at the altar of Bill James, but I do what I can to keep his respect for reasoning, credible statistics, and irreverence—in all its forms—intact.

This hasn't always been popular. But as more young writers come up behind me and the stodgier journalists retire (Bill would say "croak," but I'm a softie), this world becomes ever safer for people who enjoy a mix of words and numbers. This is true of baseball's general managers too. Most of today's under-thirty-five generation of non-playing executives, the ever-ballyhooed group including Theo Epstein of the Red Sox, Jon Daniels of the Rangers, and many others, were weaned on James' theories and show-me-the-data approach, making it a cornerstone of their management philosophies. Most anyone my age or younger involved in baseball can't help to have been influenced, willingly or not, by James and the culture he fostered. Fitzgerald once said, "A writer should write for the youth of his own generation, the critics of the next, and the schoolmasters of ever afterward." I think Bill is well on his way to fulfilling that charge.

Bill James is quite certainly the most influential baseball writer of the twentieth century; it's not even close. Yes, Dick Young was the first to insist on working the clubhouse for quotes after games. Leonard Shecter and his fellow "Chipmunks" scurrying around New York press boxes in the 1960s sent sports journalism shifting from the reverential to the sensational. And Peter Gammons' notebooks helped make him the king of multimedia. But it was Bill James, a nobody from Kansas with some sharp pencils and an even sharper wit, who rewrote how we talk, think and report about baseball. We don't ask how long Beethoven's influence will be felt in music or Newton's will be felt in science. James' impact on his field is similarly immune from half-life.

I have worked as a professional baseball scout for the last nine years and can say that I would not be where I am were it not for Bill James. I was introduced to his work while at the University of North Carolina in the early 1980s. He changed the way I viewed the game of baseball and inflamed a curiosity in me about the game that has never diminished.

Bill James was part of what drove me to become a sportswriter after college and later to continue learning about the game when I was covering the Triple-A Pawtucket Red Sox for a newspaper. Much of what pushed me over that ten-year period was the desire to find out why James' theories were not being embraced by the professional baseball world. For example, my first question when I met then Oakland Athletics scout J.P. Ricciardi, who would years later become my boss with the Toronto Blue Jays, was about sabermetrics. It was through these conversations that I learned enough about the evaluation of players to become a scout and continue my quest. And, of course, over that same period I watched James' work take hold of the industry.

I finally met Bill James the night the Red Sox clinched a playoff berth in 2003, his first season with the club and my fifth as a scout. I explained how important he had been to me and my career.

KIMBALL CROSSLEY
Baseball Scout
Gilbert, Arizona

In June of 1982, I was getting ready to graduate from Harvard. Because I was (and remain) crazy, I was also getting ready to be married two days after graduation.

I wanted my gifts to my ushers to be personalized, to reflect their likes and interests. One dear friend was, like me, an enormous baseball fan, so I went to the bookstore to look for a baseball book and found the *1982 Baseball Abstract*. I'd never heard of Bill James, but the back cover looked interesting, so I bought it.

I had a job at the time manning the dorm security desk. One night I took a novel to read during my shift, as well as the copy of the *Abstract* so that I could giftwrap it. I made the mistake of randomly looking at and reading a page in the middle of the book. I was instantly, irretrievably hooked and realized that I ABSOLUTELY HAD TO read this book IMMEDIATELY.

Problem: I was an impoverished student about to be married and giving the book as a gift. I could neither give my friend an obviously-used book nor afford to buy a replacement.

Solution: Students passing by the security desk were treated to the sight of me carefully lifting each page a minuscule amount, inserting a small mirror I found in the security desk drawer, and putting my face within two inches of that mirror so I could read the page without cracking the book's spine, knowing as I did so that my views on how a baseball team should be constructed were changing forever. I did this for hours and hours, mesmerized, wiping the fog from the mirror, reading every word on every page in one sitting. In a mirror. BACKWARDS.

MITCH FORMAN
Grants and Contracts Manager
Connecticut Division of Criminal Justice
Cheshire, Connecticut

Ten Things I Learned from Bill James

by Dave Studenmund

editor of *The Hardball Times Baseball Annual*

Remember Ken Phelps? In the 1970s and 1980s, Phelps was a slugging first baseman who didn't get a legitimate major league opportunity until he was twenty-nine years old. As Bill James wrote in the *1987 Baseball Abstract*: "Ken Phelps has been a major-league ballplayer since at least 1980, when he hit .294 with 128 walks and a slugging percentage close to .600 at AAA Omaha, a tough park for a hitter. Through 1985 he had 567 at-bats in the major leagues—one season's worth—with 40 home runs and 92 RBI."

Even after he reached the majors, Phelps never played more than 125 games in a single season. Yet he tallied a .374 on-base average and a .480 slugging percentage, and he hit 33 home runs every 500 at-bats. Think those are impressive batting stats? You should; they're roughly the same as Jose Canseco's.

Why didn't Ken Phelps get the opportunity he deserved, when he obviously could have helped many major league teams? Well, you see, he had weaknesses: He didn't hit lefties as well as righties; he was a poor fielder; he wasn't fast; and he didn't hit for average (a lifetime batting average of .239). Major league talent evaluators chose to focus on his weaknesses instead of his awesome production. They played guys like Henry Cotto instead, and they hurt their teams.

I knew about this at the time. I saw what was going on. Not because I was particularly smart or anything, but because I read Bill James' annual *Baseball Abstracts*. James created a campaign for underappreciated players, called the Ken Phelps All-Stars, to emphasize the obvious talent right in front of baseball management's noses.

That's just one example of what Bill James did and how he did it. James unearthed wrongs in major league ball, wrote about them with insight and eloquence, and opened doors in the minds of baseball fans like me. He changed the way many of us watch and think about the game, and I will be grateful to him forever.

***

It's been over twenty years since I read my first *Abstract*, and I've probably forgotten twenty times more than I can recall from his books. But I'd like to list the following ten lessons, ten things Bill James taught to those who would listen, ten things I hope I never forget.

1. Experts don't always know what's going on.

Bill James disdains clichés. He looks beyond the preconceptions and biases of Major League Baseball and dares to question them. In many ways, James was a blogger before the World Wide Web was invented. He was a baseball fan, an outsider willing to ask simple, naïve questions. He simply wanted to write about his passion and to reach others with a similar passion. Imagine what he could have done with a *Baseball Abstract Blog*.

James questioned those who said there was no audience for the *Baseball Abstract*. In the *1985 Abstract*, he described the typical reaction of publishers to his idea: "If I wrote that Juan Samuel was a great player because his stolen bases were so enormously valuable, that was OK; if I began by asking 'How important are stolen bases to an offense?' then the audience wasn't interested in that kind of stuff."

James didn't accept that bit of accepted wisdom, and he plunged ahead. Thank goodness he did.

2. Things that are secondary can be primary.

Among his many statistical contributions, James invented something called runs created. It was based on the simple premise that the combination of on-base average and slugging percentage can predict a team's runs scored and/or an individual's contribution to his team's runs.

There are many other "run estimation" formulas. In fact, James has updated runs created itself about a gajillion times. But he did more than anyone to help people understand that the most-frequently referenced batting stats—such as batting average and RBIs—while not really meaningless, just aren't that meaningful.

Along the way, he invented something called secondary average, which is essentially the opposite of batting average. He took everything that isn't included in batting average (total bases without singles, walks, and stolen bases) and divided them by at-bats. It was a crazy, silly idea with no innate logic, unlike runs created, but James used it to celebrate the skills that baseball fans tend to overlook. Secondary average was a Bill James "cause," like his Ken Phelps' All-Stars. The point was made.

3. The only stat that really matters is the win.

James was mostly interested in runs scored and runs allowed, because they lead to the most important stat of all: wins. In fact, he

Bill James taught me how to think objectively, not just regarding baseball but also when it comes to politics, social science, the law, and my own profession. He taught me that facts are irrelevant without context. Quite frankly, if Bill James wrote a book about peanut butter, I would buy it immediately.

TOM RATHKAMP
Senior Technical Writer
Cedarburg, Wisconsin

invented something called the Pythagorean Formula, which combined a team's runs scored and allowed him to predict its wins and losses.

James always wanted to take the next logical leap: players create runs, runs lead to wins, so you should be able to allocate wins to players. And after many years of tinkering, he unveiled a book titled *Win Shares* based on a new statistic he developed. Win Shares are a very complex series of calculations (it takes over 100 pages to describe the system) that allocate a "share" of each team's wins to each ballplayer—including pitchers, batters and fielders. As a system, Win Shares has its flaws, but the creation and publication of *Win Shares* has helped many baseball fans understand the feasibility and primacy of basing an individual player's stats on his contribution to his team's wins.

In typical Jamesian style, he found some new insights he didn't expect along the way. For instance, Win Shares revealed that one reason center fielder Richie Ashburn's fielding stats looked so good is that he played behind some of the most extreme flyball staffs of all time. Even when conjuring up a statistic, Bill James discovers new insights.

4. Context matters.

So much of what we pay attention to in baseball is dependent on context:

- Outfielders will catch more balls behind pitchers who give up more flyballs, and vice versa for infielders.
- A pitcher's wins and losses depend a great deal on his team's offense.
- Some batters hit lefties better than righties, or righties better than lefties.
- Vice versa for pitchers.
- Ballparks can have a tremendous impact on a ballgame, something that became obvious to everyone when the Rockies opened for business in 1993 and the new Great American Ballpark in Cincinnati opened in 2005.
- A home run was worth more in 1968 than in 1998, because they were less frequent.
- Batters will have more RBIs if they bat with more runners on base.

What this means is that when you compare players in different eras, against different teams, from different situations and ballparks, you should take nothing at face value. Bill James rarely takes anything at face value. That is his nature. Nearly every James' essay that explores context has taught me something.

5. Don't settle for the easy answer.

In 1986, both the *Baseball Abstract* and the *Elias Baseball Analyst* addressed the question of what seems to make a Red Sox team successful. In the *Abstract*, James analyzed the seven most successful teams in Red Sox history and came to this conclusion (the capital letters are his): "IT TRIVIALIZES HISTORY to imagine that we can reduce it to a few simple lessons that will guide us through our own times. I think that one can accurately generalize this far about the successful Red Sox teams: that they have had a good mix of left-handed and right-handed hitters, that they have probably had less power than most people imagine, that they have scored a great many runs by hitting for average, hitting a lot of doubles and their share of home runs, that their pitching staffs have had good to exceptional control but (because of the park) have had only average earned run averages, that they have had some speed in center field but little otherwise, that they have had some left-handed pitching but not a lot."

As I recall (I threw away my copy), *The Elias Baseball Analyst* also analyzed the most successful Red Sox teams, ran a regression, found that home runs were positively correlated with winning. Their recommendation: The Red Sox should stack every position with lots of home run hitters. Unlike Elias, Bill James didn't settle for easy answers.

Many years later, John Henry and the Red Sox would hire Bill James. I wonder if they read those two essays?

6. Relief pitching is kind of controversial.

Bill James has written three essays about major league bullpens:

- In the first *Historical Baseball Abstract* (published in 1985), he included a fine background article called "A History of Relief Pitching."
- In the *Bill James Guide to Managers* (published in 1997), he wrote an essay called "The Modern Bullpen," which covered much of the same ground but from a managerial strategy perspective. His conclusion was that bullpen strategy will keep changing and that someday it may revert to previous patterns in which fewer pitchers were used for longer stints.

- In the *New Historical Baseball Abstract* (published in 2001), he wrote a technical piece called "Valuing Relievers," which concluded that relief aces should be used more often in tie games and for multiple innings. Currently, they are almost always used when their team is ahead in the ninth inning only.

The Boston press jumped all over James in 2003 when the Red Sox failed to sign a big-name reliever, suggesting that they were following a James-inspired blueprint to run a "bullpen by committee." Maybe he suggested that approach to someone somewhere, but he didn't suggest it in any of his bullpen articles. The truth is, however, that relief aces obviously should be used more often in the late innings of tie games and probably used more often for more than just the ninth inning. What is so upsetting about that? Bill James isn't the only guy who can see that.

> Some people like to read science fiction, while others like to read romance novels. I prefer to curl up with Bill James' new book on baseball each and every fall.
>
> **RICH SNYDER**
> CPA
> Milwaukee, Wisconsin

7. We still have a lot to learn about baseball managers.

What makes a baseball manager effective? Who's good and who's bad? Why has Joe Torre been such a good manager with the Yankees, when he was so bad with the Mets?

Bill James has spent a lot of time thinking and writing about these sorts of questions. In fact, the *Guide to Baseball Managers* is my favorite James book. In it, James explored new ways of advancing the manager "conundrum" and wrote many excellent chapters on the evolution of managers and baseball strategy.

It is unfortunate that James' impact in this area hasn't been nearly as powerful as it has been in other areas and that the subject of baseball's field generals remains primarily a matter of opinion, with no publicly accepted framework for discussion. I suppose that's the nature of the beast, but it wouldn't surprise me to see James tackle this subject again.

8. Baseball statistics want to be free.

There was a war in the 1980s. It began when Bill James asked Elias for baseball scoresheets and they said no. The stats were secret or something. James responded in two ways: words and action. In the *1984 Abstract*, he published a bit of a manifesto: "In short, we as analysts of the game, or even not as analysts of the game, but as historians or record-makers or biographers or simply fans, are blocked off from the basic source of information which we need to undertake an incalculable variety of investigative studies. We need accounts; we are given summaries. We need access to an exact record of what happens. We are told that that is for the big boys, not for us measly fans. I feel this is very wrong."

In that essay, James announced something called Project Scoresheet, which would consist of an army of volunteers documenting every game, collating the stats and making them available to the public. It was a big undertaking, but Project Scoresheet worked. Games were tracked, stats were collated and reported, and new books like the *Great American Baseball Stat Book* were published.

Unfortunately, Project Scoresheet fell apart after a few years, but the quest to set baseball statistics free never did. Today, we have remarkable websites like Retrosheet.org and Baseball-Reference.com that are fantastic resources for many fans. For that, you can thank Bill James.

9. It's easy to be misunderstood.

Do you remember *Pogo*, the comic strip? *Pogo* was one of my favorite comics. Its cutting, political humor and artwork paved the way for many great contemporary comic strips, such as *Doonesbury* and *Calvin and Hobbes*.

Pogo stopped running in 1973, but it was revived for a few years in the late 1980s by the son of Walt Kelly, Pogo's creator. Kelly's son, like his father, was evidently a big baseball fan, but he didn't like Bill James. In fact, he created a *Pogo* character named "Bull James" who spouted extremely detailed and ridiculous baseball statistics, much to the consternation of the inhabitants of the Okeefenokee Swamp.

That's when I started feeling bad for Bill James. It's one thing to be ridiculed by sportswriters, but to be ridiculed in one of the best comic strips ever written? Without running for public office? That was a low blow. I like

> I have been a huge baseball fan since 1949 (age nine), and from the beginning was fascinated by baseball statistics. That was a hobby. I became a physician, and over the years realized the importance of what we now call "evidence-based medicine." My hobby and my profession have come together with the work inspired by Bill James. Books like *Moneyball* and *Baseball Inside the Numbers* are "evidence-based baseball," and proponents of this approach in both medicine and baseball are at first scorned by the traditional practitioners. It takes years to change the way people think in both areas, but sometimes I can use examples from baseball to influence physicians' thinking.
>
> **HENRY BERMAN, MD**
> Physician
> Seattle, Washington

to think that Walt Kelly himself would have been more sympathetic to Bill James' quest. After all, he is the man who wrote: "We have met the enemy and he is us." Major league execs take note.

10. It's not about the stats; it's all about baseball.

Maybe you read *Playboy* for the articles. Well, maybe not, but that was why I read the *Abstracts*. Some people seem to think that the *Abstracts* were a bunch of statistics and numbers, data tables, split stats, etc. They weren't.

The *Abstracts* were filled with words and ideas. As James said in the *1982 Abstract*, the first one published for a wide audience: "Sabermetrics does not begin with the numbers. It begins with issues. The numbers, the statistics, are not the subject of the discussion; they are not the subject of this book. The subject is baseball."

When words and ideas come together, as they often do with Bill James, you sometimes feel like Lewis and Clark, gazing out on a brand new world. Bill James has made it even more fun to be a baseball fan. I can't wait to learn ten more things from him.

I first encountered Bill James' work in the 1988 *Baseball Abstract*. Since that time, not only has his writing altered my view of the national pastime but his use of logic, historical insights, and critical analysis has also challenged me to delve deeper into all aspects of the game I love. Twenty years ago, I wouldn't question what sportswriters, broadcasters and front-office personnel would write or say. Due to James' efforts, I don't settle for trite or hackneyed phrases from talk-show hosts or agents. Along with many other folks, I now think for myself and hold my favorite team accountable for personnel acquisitions, ballpark construction, and even business decisions regarding the franchise.

More importantly, though, reading James' work has made me a better thinker. I use data differently in my career as an urban planner due to James, and his style of writing has influenced me to be more concise and forceful. Sure, I disagree with a few of his ideas, but his views have revolutionized how we all think about sports in America. He belongs in the sports writers wing of the Baseball Hall of Fame for the variety and complexity of his writing alone.

TIM ANGELL
Urban Planner
Evanston, Illinois

The Arrogance of Bill James

by Gary Huckabay

founder of Baseball Prospectus

Before I had any idea who Bill James was or what his work in base-ball analysis was about, I knew he was arrogant.

You see, there were ex-players, writers and commentators on the radio (even back in the early 1980s) who were kind enough to let me know that James was some sort of uninformed hack who never played the game and hence couldn't possibly have anything of value to offer the public when it came to understanding it. So James' very act of writing a bunch of stuff down for others to read was not merely folly but an endeavor of nearly unparalleled insolence and sedition.

At the time, I didn't grasp the importance or controversy of what James was saying in his *Baseball Abstracts*. I loved baseball, and like most fans I thought I knew pretty much everything about the game. *Of course* sacrifice bunts made sense. *Of course* Tony Armas was the best right fielder in baseball...and not just because of the hair! One of the fondest memories I have of growing up is spending a lazy week-end afternoon in the cab of our truck in the driveway at home, half dozing, listening to Bill King call A's games. I distinctly remember King commenting about recently reading a book by someone named Bill James—the same guy that I had heard criticized by some talking head on the radio earlier that season. It was several months until I actually read my first *Abstract*, and thus I began an education process that would continue for many decades, through several media and multiple teachers, and with more than a few relapses on my part.

***

Cries of "arrogance" are often the first reaction of an existing power structure to the suggestion of change. It's true not just in baseball but also in virtually every industry or enterprise, from politics to the arts. However, for the group that happens to be in power, making the decisions that actually drive the enterprise or the industry, the disquieting reality is that the true arrogance is not displayed by the upstart with the new idea but by the calcified inhabitants of the positions of power. After all, how dare someone suggest that the status quo isn't the best possible way to run things? The seminal human response to any attack is to fight back, and questioning existing authority is an implicit attack on the judgment of those in power.

> Fundamentally, Bill James made me realize that it was OK to think about baseball as an adult, the same way you think about religion, politics, art and stock options.
>
> **BARRY GORDEN**
> Technical Writer
> Portland, Oregon

And make no mistake, James' writing in the *Abstracts* were a full-frontal assault on the power structure in baseball. In our current world, where every would-be Oscar Wilde or Thomas Hobbes can invest three hours and twenty-five bucks, start a blog, and bore millions with a few keystrokes, it's easy to forget that thirty years ago there was no such echo chamber of analysis and dissent. Although people like Earnshaw Cook and

George Lindsey predated James chronologically, James was the guy who stepped forward and said, in effect, "Let's examine the way decisions are made in baseball and find out if things could be done better." Even today, a quarter of a century later, front office baseball execs are still fighting back like cornered wolverines, which should give you some idea of the level of passion and vitriol James was facing back then.

The real power of the *Baseball Abstracts* wasn't in the statistical analysis. The real power came from the fact that James was a far better writer than he was a researcher. How many people can realistically take what is, in effect, a dry, academic exercise and make it genuinely entertaining to a wide audience? It's this Jamesian skill that was essential to spreading the ideas proffered in his *Abstracts:* not just his analysis of things like Gold Glove voting, defense, and sacrifice bunts but the very idea of critically examining the status quo in the first place. There are literally millions of people in the world who can do the work of gathering and evaluating data. But the ability to make it interesting to the masses while retaining the power of the information being conveyed? That's a truly rare talent.

James' ability to make tedious data accessible and even fascinating, when combined with his intimate and iconoclastic writing style, somehow contributed to the perception that there was an arrogance to his work. The very items that made his material readable and enjoyable were often well outside the realm of strict analysis. Great drama and comedy comes from contrast, and reading dense, informational material and then suddenly coming upon James calling one player "Scott 'Will Your Sister' Leius" is great contrast; and despite being kind of an easy laugh, it was pretty damn funny at the time. His poking fun at Alfredo Griffin's baserunning misadventures is akin to shooting fish in a really narrow barrel, but it does tend to put the people who hired and managed poor Mr. Griffin on the defensive. Great writers and comedians poke fun at power, and when power's mistakes are on such magnificent display as they are in baseball, it makes for two things—great entertainment and pissed authority figures. Both of those phenomena contribute to polarization: The pissed authority figures don't tend to move in your direction, and the general population starts paying more attention to what you're saying, pissing off the authority figures to an even greater extent.

***

The story of Bill James' impact on baseball is paralleled in many, if not most, other industries. The general formula has been laid out in absurd numbers of management books and mediocre MBA seminars, so doing so once more here isn't going to hurt anything. Here's the over-simplified straw man of a process:

1. Outsider (often hirsute) questions the decision-making process and prowess of existing authorities in industry, presents alternative methods of approaching industry or task at hand. This may include new methods of measuring success, changing the basic way an industry works, or asking for objective measurement of performance.

2. Threatened hierophants point out that outsider can't possibly have all the information necessary to understand the complex nature of what's really going on, because all that information is locked here in the temple, and by the way is not really written down anywhere, per se.

3. Outsider presents evidence of new approach or product, and measurement system that demonstrates equality or superiority of new approach. (Note: actual superiority to status quo is optional here.)

4. Hierophants either clamp down and crush the rebellion like Travis Hafner facing a Jose Lima "fast" ball, pay off the insider with acceptance into the Inner Circle, or are usurped by a raging tide of converted believers and/or facts.

For example, Bill Gates had the nerve to suggest that computer software shouldn't be developed by and for a bunch of information-hoarding homebrew computer geeks and should actually be bought and paid for. Mohandas Gandhi believed that alternative strategies could achieve the independence that traditional warfare had failed to deliver to the people of India. Or, on a level that more people can grasp, Joe Francis of Mantra Films thought that drunken frat boys would pay millions of dollars to watch drunken co-eds flash their boobs in *Girls Gone Wild*. (Really, the innovation there was the direct distribution channel and the leveraging of a cultural shift that has dramatically reduced our average cost of selling out.) The competitors or opposition to these innovative people cry "arrogance," not necessarily as a tactic but because they believe it.

In real life, and other industries, the final result is usually a combination of all the items in #4, and the biggest risk is often that the outsider grows as calcified and stubborn—or arrogant, if you will—as the insiders he or she once railed against.

***

I believe Bill James is the most influential person in baseball with respect to how insiders and serious fans think about the game since Branch Rickey. He challenged long-held consensus viewpoints by researching such issues and presenting indisputable evidence to the contrary in many cases.

As the son of a baseball writer and executive, I grew up eating, sleeping, breathing and playing baseball well before James published his first book. However, my knowledge of the game took on new meaning after I was introduced to his astute analysis and writing. His wit and wisdom are unmatched in the annals of baseball, and I feel fortunate that I have been able to extend my admiration for the man into a personal relationship that I cherish.

RICH LEDERER
Baseball Analyst
Long Beach, California

I think Bill James deserves an awful lot of credit for moving baseball forward. His published baseball research has been good, but it hasn't been anything close to infallible. Still, he's put it out there, asked the right questions, and inspired a couple generations of people to stand up and question authority—not in the 1960s-patchouli-oil-and-macramé fashion but in the spirit of "Hell yes, I want to compete, and I want to win." I've been lucky enough to work with a bunch of really talented and energetic people in my career, and a surprising number of them (even outside *Baseball Prospectus*) were shaped in large part by Bill James' writing and approach to the task of improving baseball. And that's perhaps what's scared the powers that be enough to use the term "arrogant" to begin with. Of course James was threatening to the baseball establishment and particularly the sports press. Given the choice of working in an environment where accountability was virtually nonexistent and working in a world where every decision is subject to constant second-guessing and evaluation, who'd choose the latter?

Ultimately, however, I think James' impact has been far greater outside of baseball than within it. He helped shape the culture of innovation in our society that's been responsible for many positive improvements. (I won't blame him for *Girls Gone Wild*.) James' body of work, particularly the *Abstracts,* is a testament to the courage needed to stand up and tell truth to power. It's strange to think that accountability is often the result of the introduction and examination of new ideas, but it's what often follows. That's not a new lesson—leaders of all stripes have known it for centuries. Or, more simply put, "Ideas are more powerful than guns. We would not let our enemies have guns, why should we let them have ideas?" That's what Stalin thought, and he knew a thing or two about suppressing the threat posed by upstarts.

Thankfully, in baseball, the stakes are slightly lower.

I first learned about Bill James from a short article in *Sports Illustrated* in the early 1980s and was soon shocked and thrilled to see him systematically debunk so many of our national pastime's previously unquestioned articles of faith. Longing for the publication of the annual *Abstract* immediately became a true rite of spring for me. Who would have thought that bunting (successfully) could take you out of so many big innings, or that 60 stolen bases might be of absolutely no consequence if you were caught stealing twenty times, or that Ozzie Smith's glove wasn't really saving Whitey Herzog 100 runs per year?

For me, James' finest moment was when he published his Jeter vs. Everett essay in John Dewan's *The Fielding Bible* last year. Over the years, Jeter's fielding accolades, let alone his couple of Gold Gloves, never seemed quite right to me. Balls that were hit with medium speed seemed to wind up in the outfield, as Jeter took one step toward the ball and then gave up. Was his "patented jump and throw move" really something that other shortstops could not do, or was it something that they didn't need to do? Were his great over-the-shoulder catches products of Willie Mays-like instincts, or was he cheating in to an unreasonably shallow position? As a lifelong Yankee hater, I needed to know.

James didn't merely reconfigure the way in which I watched the game; he stripped away "Captain Derek's" aura of infallibility to the point that Jeter's deficiencies have now been acknowledged by everyone from *Sports Illustrated for Kids* to a couple (but not all) of my hard-headed Yankee-fan buddies.

MICHAEL K. EIDMAN
Attorney
Englewood, New Jersey

Although I have never met Bill James, he is one of the primary people I credit in helping me become a professor of engineering. In the summer of 1984, before my senior year in high school, I read my first *Baseball Abstract*. The book opened up a new world to me, detailing the importance and intricacies of not only statistical analysis but also of the management of people and organizations. I studied the book, learning more about the game than I could ever have imagined.

When I got to college, I thought that I wanted to be an electrical engineer. But after hearing a talk on industrial engineering, a field made up of the study of—among other things—statistics, optimization, ergonomics, organizational behavior, economics and management, I knew that I wanted to study and improve systems involving people. In the back of my mind, I was thinking that most if not all of these topics had first been introduced to me by Bill James.

I earned a bachelor's degree in industrial engineering and moved on to graduate school to continue my studies. Along the way, I proposed a dissertation topic of developing optimization models for use in baseball. The topic was dismissed as frivolous. Still, I finished my Ph.D. in industrial engineering and have been teaching at Hofstra University ever since. I profess to anyone who will listen that industrial engineering is an ideal background for a career in baseball management. To the delight of most of my students, I weave baseball into the teaching of virtually all of my courses. My students and I can thank Bill James for helping us not only *think about* baseball or engineering or life but also *study and learn* more about baseball and engineering and life.

RICHARD J. PUERZER
Chairperson and Professor of Engineering
Hofstra University
Metuchen, New Jersey

Prove It

by John Thorn

co-author of *The Hidden Game of Baseball* and *Total Baseball*

I remember the boyhood arguments about who was the better New York center fielder. Voices and gorges would rise until one of us would declare the matter settled in favor of Willie, Mickey, or the Duke: "Because I said so!" Then another kid would be sure to howl, "Oh yeah? Prove it!" And wielding such cudgels as home runs, batting averages, RBIs, and World Series rings, we schoolyard scientists would set about to settle nothing at all. The debate would be set aside to rage another day, with as much heat and as little light.

Baseball writers of that day were no better than large schoolboys. Perhaps today the practitioners, and I include myself, remain case studies in arrested development. But while the challenge to "prove it" may still stump us, we ask better questions these days, we debate at a more rational level, and we have a healthy disrespect for received opinion and official wisdom. For this raised station we may thank Bill James.

James and I have known each other for more than twenty years as friendly rivals. Although we issued competing reference works, he graciously praised the books I created with Pete Palmer, and I included his writing in my various anthologies. Prefacing a selection from his *Baseball Abstract* in *The Armchair Book of Baseball* in 1985, I orated: "It is not too much to say that James has revolution-ized the way fans think about the game and the way professionals write about it." The uncommon sense of sabermetrics—which might be said to encompass skepticism, reason, empiricism and rigor—has weaned podunk scribes and sclerotic columnists from the "gee whiz" approach to baseball. (Now if we could only get them to do more with their daily coverage than hover around the clubhouse foraging for quotes!)

Reassessing James' contribution to baseball writers, executives, managers and fans two decades later, I have come to believe that it extends beyond his useful methodologies. Sabermetrics is not prin-cipally a toolkit but an old-fashioned habit of mind, freshly applied to a simple yet enduringly complex game. I learned from his early work to think about the game more critically. Recalling the count-ing and averaging approach of the stat tables I included in *The Relief Pitcher* in 1979, I shudder. But his singular benefit to my thinking and writing, especially in a nonstatistical vein, has been his interest in asking childish questions and challenging conventional wisdom. ("Prove it!") If everybody believes something to be true, that doesn't make it true—indeed, as in the stock market, the direction of the herd is a good sign to go the other way.

***

Bill James has been like the boy who had the courage or naiveté to point out that the splendor of the emperor's new clothes was a sham, a lie agreed upon by everyone else. This clear view, of course, brought scorn upon his head from the establishment, even after Michael Lewis' *Moneyball* celebrated the mainstreaming of his former heresies. When James joined the front office of the Boston Red Sox, owner John Henry said, "I assume the inherent bias against him within baseball will increase now that he has taken sides." It did, as Red Sox failures ("bullpen by committee") were attributed to him and successes (the 2004 World Championship) were ascribed to others.

In the 2004 edition of *Total Baseball,* which included James' Win Shares as well as Pete Palmer's Linear Weights, Alan Schwarz and I named Bill the 40th most important person in the history of baseball (flanked at 39 by Alex Rodriguez and at 41 by Sandy Alderson). We wrote: "For the past twenty-five years, baseball has been in the throes of a statistics revolution. No one person was more responsible for this than Bill James, the most influential baseball writer of the twentieth century." (Oh, how we'd like to blue-pencil "throes" now!)

> I look forward to Bill James' enshrinement at Cooperstown.
>
> **MITCH MELNICK**
> Sports Director and PM Drive Host
> The Team 990 Radio
> Montreal, Ontario

We further opined, "He also was a fantastic writer, funny and always irreverent." To that I would now add "stubborn," not in the sense that he would hold on to a notion if outside evidence or personal reconsideration made it suspect but in the tenacity he exhibited before organized baseball's professed indifference, institutional scorn, and often shocking animus. James had the courage of his convictions and curried no favor. Along Publishers Row he was legendary for his resistance to editors' blandishments to soften his judgments or pretty up his prose. If there were to be errors in judgment or lapses in taste, they would be *his,* dammit.

Stubborn is a good thing for a writer or thinker or person to be.

***

In 1984 when Pete Palmer and I wrote *The Hidden Game of Baseball*, we felt driven to explain and reveal some mysteries in plain sight (if one trusted the numbers rather than one's eyes): For example, those backhand stops and cross-body throws to first didn't make Frank Taveras a great fielder, if over the course of a season he reached fewer balls than a league-average shortstop; Cal Ripken's year-end total chances belied his seemingly narrow range and few flashy plays. Five years later, in the first edition of *Total Baseball*, we wrote: "For the veteran fan as well as for Major League Baseball, new ideas, new statistics, and new discoveries that dispute long-held verities (Ty Cobb's hit total, Hoss Radbourn's number of victories in 1884, etc.) may represent a challenge to tradition and thus a threat to the very soul of baseball, its pride in anachronism. Bernard Malamud wrote, 'The whole history of baseball has the quality of mythology.'"

In recent years as my interest grew in the earliest instances of baseball (pre-1860, loosely termed "protoball"), I felt more affinity for the game's mythology than its verifiable fact. Studying what people believe to be true is often far more interesting than ascertaining what may actually be true, for even generally accepted falsehoods (the Abner Doubleday concoction, for example) reveal much about the hopes of an age.

I had felt myself pulling away from statistics. While I still believed that numbers could reveal things about the game that were invisible to the naked eye, my own eyes had glazed over as the combination of fantasy baseball and mathematical arcana conspired to squeeze the life from the game I loved. Baseball viewed through statistics seemed less like play and more like work—"earnest," in Johan Huizinga's useful opposite to "playful."

In the spring of 2006, it turned out that Bill James was unable to deliver his promised keynote speech at the SABR Regional Conference in Boston, which was to have a sabermetric theme. I was asked to address the assembled statisticians in his stead and, despite my demurrals that I was neither a sabermetrician nor a crowd-pleasing substitute for the headline act, I agreed to fill in. I prepared a speech that was publicized in advance of the meeting as "Zanzibar Cats," signaling my direction to those who knew the line from Thoreau's *Walden*: "It is not worth the while to go round the world to count the cats in Zanzibar."

Taking the podium, I began: "My sabermetric achievements lie behind me rather than ahead, and, echoing Paul Gallico's *Farewell to Sport*, I think I am now about ready to say, 'Farewell to Stats.' For a whole generation of fans and fantasy players, stats have begun to outstrip story and that is a sad thing.... For this I could blame Bill James, Pete Palmer, and maybe myself a little too. The press has often termed me a sabermetrician and placed me in the company of my betters. In fact I never was a statistician...." Here I began to sound like Nixon.

I proceeded to provide naptime for many in the audience as I ranged over and through bat-and-ball antiquity as well as the history of sporting statistics. To lash them back awake I said, "Baseball fans of earlier generations had fewer statistics at their disposal, but a simpler game perhaps had no need of them. Our forebears' very lack of stats may have made them more sociable and more cooperative enthusiasts than those of today, made possessive and isolated by fantasy baseball and constant numerical evaluation of their favorites."

***

"Farewell to Stats" indeed. But maybe not to sabermetrics, I thought, whose habits of mind daily inform my historical research into an era of baseball that knew no statistics.

I had already commenced writing this tribute reminiscence of Bill James when a note from SABR's Ryan Chamberlain popped up on its Nineteenth Century Baseball listserv: "I've been discussing the origins of the game a lot lately with various people and I'm wondering…does a chronology exist for the topic, 'How Did We Come to Understand Baseball History?' Where do you start and end on something like this…with Chadwick?… the Seymours?…and then work your way outward? The only analogy I can think of off the top of my head is Sigmund Freud to modern psychology. Even though many of his ideas are archaic by today's standards, he certainly was responsible for making psychology popular."

Christopher Green responded: "What we really need is not merely a popularizer…but a person who also creates a new and powerful vocabulary for talking about, and ultimately for analyzing, some activity that had not been considered worthy of much analysis to that point. But it can't be too technical (e.g., Newton) or it fails to capture the popular aspect of Chadwick's achievement. No one strikingly similar to Chadwick in these ways comes to mind."

I dashed off a one-sentence reply: "Sounds to me like Bill James."

Bill James didn't teach me only the vital importance of on-base percentage or the relative unimportance of bunts and steals. More importantly, he showed how to approach problems. Not only problems in the baseball world but problems in *the* world. He time and again not only presented his readers with Aha! moments but also documented how he got there, inspiring all of us who could see problems but didn't always understand how to grapple with them effectively. His approach: Frame a question so that it can be answered; figure out what you need to know to answer it; get the information, play with it, and let it marinate as long as you can; draw a conclusion and question it; redraw your conclusion; and finally, write it up in compelling prose. Sometimes that means entering the problem through a little crack and wedging it open to reveal its inner parts; sometimes it means being willing to risk staking out a difficult position; and sometimes it means blowing the whole damn thing up so you can get rid of the biases, blinders and notions that blocked you from seeing the thing for what it is. Was Bill James the first to think like this? To use thought experiments? To follow the lead of curiosity toward a fulfilling and engrossing end? No. But in our time, who else in any discipline has demonstrated how to think, really think, about knotty problems in such a public, accessible and nonacademic way? James the thinker, populist and writer did it time and again. It's what made him dangerous to the baseball establishment and what has endeared him to his readers.

Turning baseball's conventional wisdom upside down, that's the least of what Bill James has accomplished. Exhorting me and a lot of other folks to value thoughtfulness over automaton activity—and oftentimes showing us how to go about the kind of deep thinking he advocated—that's the real stuff of his revolution.

ERIC CHALEK
Promotions Copywriter
York, Maine

James, Tenace, McGraw and Kluszewski

by Hal Richman

founder and CEO of the Strat-O-Matic Game Company

I invented Strat-O-Matic Baseball, the board game, back in 1961, when Bill James was still a twelve-year-old kid. I knew that baseball was the greatest game in the world, and I also knew that baseball lent itself to statistical analysis because of its long history and the way it is played and documented.

I was right then, and I'm right now. Bill James has proved just how right.

James, working at the outset with only official baseball statistical data, successfully revised the thinking of fans and baseball executives alike on many of baseball's axioms and assumptions. Rebuffed by the baseball clubs and the league statisticians, James continued unraveling many of the statistical mysteries of our national pastime. His efforts attracted others to his cause and eventually led to the development of non-league statistical bureaus that enable all fans to have a better understanding of the game.

However, it is one thing to influence the thinking of baseball fans and another to influence the thinking of baseball management. James is beginning to do that as well.

***

When I was a boy, a teenager, and a young man, I was a Yankee fan. I invested time, energy and emotion into being a fan. But as I became an adult, changes in the game such as the advent of free agency pushed the fan in me aside. I was becoming estranged from the game.

Then I discovered the *Baseball Abstracts*. I had always been interested in analyzing baseball, but Bill James' annual book made my interest blossom. The parochial outlook of a fan was transformed into the more critical outlook of an analyst. Being an engineer, quantitative investigations of baseball fit right in with my technical background. I discovered a new place for baseball in my life thanks to Bill James.

RALPH CAOLA
Business Owner
Troy, New York

If you played the Strat-O-Matic baseball game in the 1960s or 1970s, you may have been subconsciously aware that the batting average statistic was not a good representation of a player's hitting abilities. The most obvious Strat-O-Matic player card example was the Oakland A's catcher, Gene Tenace. Though Tenace batted only .211 in 1974 (47 points below the league average), good Strat-O-Matic players realized he nevertheless got on base 14% more than the average American Leaguer and scored 12% higher in the on-base-plus-slugging category. This was quite evident when viewing Tenace's Strat-O-Matic player card, a text graphic of his offensive abilities. His home run power was more than twice the league's average, and his 106 walks dominated the card. He was a "sleeping giant favorite pick" in many Strat-O-Matic leagues. If Billy Beane played Strat-O-Matic in 1974 (when *he* was only twelve years old), I am sure he would have picked Tenace for his team. Beane, of course, became general manager of Oakland and utilized many of James' theories in formulating his roster, as documented in Michael Lewis' great book *Moneyball*. With few dollars to spend, Beane's Oakland teams have been able to compete favorably with the big-buck teams because of his utilization of many of the ideas propounded by James and his disciples.

It must be pointed out that Strat-O-Matic only displayed this kind of information on ballplayers on our cards; we did not comment on it. But Bill James sure did, especially in his famous *Abstracts* that revolutionized the game. For example, he made the baseball world (fans and management alike) consciously accept the fact that the batting average by itself was a poor measurement of a player's offensive strengths. Prior to James, a player hitting .300 with few walks and little power was greatly respected by the baseball community. James' efforts downgraded significantly batting average's icon status and placed it in its proper perspective. Batting average is now seen for what it is: one element (albeit an important one) of the on-base-plus-slugging combination.

Like batting average, the value of the sacrifice bunt was an accepted axiom in baseball from the very beginnings of the sport. Baseball as it was played in Pittsfield, Massachusetts, in 1791 and for many decades thereafter was a low-scoring game. The lack of power by most players made the bunt an important offensive weapon. Managers throughout baseball history accepted the use of the sacrifice bunt in certain situations as the gospel truth, and one generation of managers handed this philosophy down to the next generation of managers. This continued until one man—Bill James—hammered away at this theory, eventually proving that giving up an out in many instances (by bunting) reduces your run potential significantly.

The same can be said of the stolen base, particularly attempting to steal second base. In the early part of the twentieth century, steals were attempted frequently. The 1911 season, for example, saw the average major league team steal over 212 bases in a 154-game schedule or 1.38 per game. Strat-O-Matic researched and created a set of player cards for 1911, however, and our research indicated that a ridiculously low 55% of the steals attempted were successful. James' current research indicates that anything below a 67% safe percentage on steals is counter-productive. If his research results had been available in 1911, perhaps Hall of Fame manager John McGraw's New York Giants would not have stolen 347 bases that year and five of his players would have not stolen 38 or more as they did. They might have realized that they were making too many outs getting caught stealing! (Another example of James' influence involves stealing third base. Attempting to steal third base was always thought to be a precarious move, prior to James' findings. It turns out that good base stealers actually have a higher success rate attempting to steal third base rather than second base.)

***

I have always thought that the major area of difficulty for James was in quantifying fielding. Prior to his efforts, fielding percentage was considered the only acceptable way of judging a player's fielding ability. Baseball fans and management knew that fielding percentage was a suspect statistic, but it was considered to be the best defensive measure available. Here was the problem: A player with limited range—such as Ted Kluszewski—would often make few errors and therefore would have a pretty good fielding percentage. But in fact anyone who bothered to watch a game knew that Kluszewski, an excellent hitter, was defensively challenged. He was a large man with little mobility.

James' earliest attempts to measure fielding used what he called the "range factor," which is still a highly regarded method of measuring defense. In fact, his initial findings clashed with who was winning Major League Baseball's Gold Glove Awards. Two players in particular aggravated James— shortstop Larry Bowa and center fielder Garry Maddox, both of them Phillies who won several Gold Gloves. However, neither player had decent range ratings and thus earned criticism from James. James felt the Gold Glove choices were based on batting ability and fielding reputations acquired without statistical analysis.

Strat-O-Matic has disagreed with James' criticism of the Gold Glove awards for the most part. We feel they are fairly accurate choices, although it was certainly the case that some undeserving players have received the award over the years. It is true that a fielder's reputation can linger and may provide him with an additional Gold Glove or two that maybe someone else should have won. And we also feel that when there is no clear-cut defensive favorite at a position it is OK if batting ability becomes a factor in the choice. If there are two great defensive third basemen, for example, and one hits .250 and the other hits .350, why not give the Gold Glove to the better all-around player? In general, we believe

Bill James more validated my view of baseball than changed it. He enabled me to finally crystallize in my mind why I became a baseball fanatic as a child. It is because baseball has always been the most objectively analyzed and quantified human activity on the planet. Bill James raised the bar on that objective analysis to a level much higher than anyone else has, before or since.

MAJ. GENERAL LARRY TAYLOR
USMC (retired)
Atlanta, Georgia

that anywhere from 14 to 16 of the 18 annual awards go to formidable defensive players who deserve the award.

Recently, however, James collaborated with John Dewan on an entire book devoted to fielding ability, titled *The Fielding Bible*. It took into account range factor, errors that shouldn't have been made and difficult plays that were, and team defensive ability. It certainly was a step in the right direction, but in my opinion it still falls short of a true defensive evaluation of many players. Still, I quibble. It is very possible that in the future Bill James will come up with the perfect statistical fielding system. I wouldn't put anything past him at this point.

I have only touched on a few of James' concepts that have revolutionized the statistical world of baseball. It is impossible to estimate the number of books, articles, and mathematical theories that have been made available to the public by other writers who have been stimulated by James' work. I'm not sure that places like ESPN or the myriad of sports websites or fantasy leagues would exist the way they do today if he had not come along. Even more importantly, I am not sure baseball would even be played the way it is today if it were not for Bill James. Many of baseball's front offices now include a statistical analyst—most notably the Boston Red Sox, where Bill James himself took the job right before the Red Sox won the World Series in 2004.

Hmmm!

Bill James changed the informational dynamics of bas information he analyzes has always been available, bu never before codified until he blended math and basel creative, dynamic fashion.

Does it work? You bet. But not always.

In Milwaukee, at the 2003 SABR Convention, Bill told the assembled audience, "I will bet you that at tomorrow's Cubs-White Sox game ne catcher will catch a foul ball in foul territory." He went on to relate how the redesign of parks had reduced the playing area available to catch foul balls. In short, the vision of the catcher throwing off his mask, circlin under a pop foul, and snaring it in the catcher's mitt was fading away because of explainable reasons.

At the next day's game at Wrigley Field, of course, the game was not two innings old when the Cubs' catcher caught a pop foul. Which proves another point that Bill James emphasizes: There are always exceptions to the rule, which is what makes baseball so overwhelmingly human and fun to follow.

ROD CABORN
Public Relations Executive
Winter Park, Florida

Selling My Soul to Bill James

by Sam Walker

sports columnist for *The Wall Street Journal*
and author of *Fantasyland*

Here is my first impression of George William James: I thought he was a monumental windbag.

It's not that I'd met the guy or read more than seven lines from one of his essays—I hadn't. It wasn't the substance of anything Bill James had postulated that made me want to poke out my eyeballs—it was the fact that he existed at all. In 1985 or thereabouts, the idea of some bearded crank from Nebraska (or was it Idaho?) lobbing typewritten hand grenades at baseball men of unimpeachable genius—like Sparky Anderson of my beloved Detroit Tigers—was something akin to high treason. If I had seen Bill James at the ballpark back then, I would have pelted him in the head with a nacho.

There were many reasons for this teenage aversion of mine. I wasn't what one might call a fan of math, for starters. And as the leadoff hitter for the much-heralded American Heating & Cooling youth summer-league baseball team, I had an image to uphold. But the big reason I hated this guy wasn't ideological. It was personal. Bill James had brainwashed my father.

From the moment my dad discovered James' *Baseball Abstract,* watching ballgames with the old man had become a thorough pain in the ass. His tolerance for baseless statements about baseball was so small that if the fat old sportswriters didn't make him steam with rage every morning their blow-dried cousins, the sportscasters, never failed to finish the job. A lot of times he tried to tone it down around my brother and me, but it didn't always work. If ever I volunteered that I "liked" a ballplayer, I could expect to hear a ten-minute treatise on all the reasons the guy was overrated and how he really ought to be benched in favor of Johnny Grubb.

My dad's infatuation with Bill James wasn't doing anything for my future in the major leagues, either. While my father never declined to play catch in the street with my brother and me, or to throw us popups and grounders until the stitches in the ball were unraveling, I'd never been able to tell if this was something he enjoyed or did out of obligation. But after he sold his soul to Bill James, the answer was plainly obvious.

The enthusiasm he put into keeping newfangled "stats" on the Tigers or having baseball arguments at parties with his friends didn't translate to the street. When he read one of those books, he'd have a dopey smile on his face and, on some occasions, he'd laugh out loud. Playing catch wasn't a chore for him, exactly, but compared to this new activity, it obviously paled.

This was the moment Bill James and I became mortal enemies. Here was my poor dad, just a nice guy who loved baseball, transformed into a statistical cyborg. He'd traded the joys of playing this game with a mitt and a ball for the cold comfort of a cheesy book. Someday, somehow, I swore, I would have my revenge.

***

It wasn't until 2004 that I finally figured out a way to do this. My plan was to take a leave from my job as a sports columnist for *The Wall Street Journal* to write a book called *Fantasyland*. The topic of this book was my bid to win Tout Wars, the nation's toughest expert Rotisserie baseball league.

It's not that I'd turned the corner and embraced the culture of statistics that makes fantasy baseball run. To the contrary, I'd never played fantasy baseball or fantasy football or even fantasy beach volleyball. As a sports columnist who had access to a press pass, I was convinced that I could beat all the Bill James disciples who populated this league by doing nothing more than hanging around in the clubhouse to get to know the "character" of the players on my team and by collecting the impressions of professional scouts and managers. Here, I thought, was my chance to prove that numbers, no matter how cleverly manipulated, couldn't tell you as much about a ballplayer's potential as a little firsthand knowledge from people who'd actually played baseball for a living.

Bill James' commitment to a career as baseball's statistical maven derived from his days as a student at the University of Kansas. It was in Lawrence that he and a group of students and friends became absorbed in playing Ball Park Baseball, a tabletop game whose realism and sophistication whetted his appetite to make use of statistics to better understand the major league game as played on the field. That his talent matched his ambition in this highly complex business is a testimony to his facile mind, unique intellect, and singular dedication to a great sport.

CHARLES F. SIDMAN
Dean Emeritus
College of Liberal Arts and Sciences
University of Florida
Gainesville, Florida

Now that Bill James, not to mention some of my competitors in Tout Wars, were getting legitimate jobs as statistical consultants to major-league teams, I was determined to prove that all their hyper-intellectual ideas didn't amount to a pile of sanitary socks.

Baseball, like other large and powerful organizations such as government, religion, and the media, would prefer to keep us ignorant of the mechanics of how things actually work and focus our attention on the magic, mysteries and platitudes instead. They want us to rely on faith instead of knowledge. Bill James has been the single most important force in demystifying baseball performance analysis for me and many of my generation. Perhaps he can become a governmentrician now and demystify that institution for us as well? Na-a-ah! Not nearly as much fun.

CHUCK HILDEBRANDT
Online Marketing
Chicago, Illinois

In the middle of this exercise, on July 8, 2004, I found myself sitting along the third-base line at Philadelphia's new ballpark along with five new acquaintances, one of whom was Bill James. I'd come to the game at the invitation of Steve Moyer, the president of Baseball Info Solutions—a Pennsylvania statistics braintrust that provides elaborate data for major league teams like the Boston Red Sox. Bill James, an old friend and collaborator of the company's founder, John Dewan, had come to check on the company's progress. Moyer, one of my Tout Wars competitors, said he thought it might be fun for me to meet James, not just because it might help save me from being such a Paleolithic dimwit but because he thought it would help me better understand what made him, and everyone else in Tout Wars, tick.

So while I came to the game with a notebook and a tape recorder with the stated purpose of studying the behavior of a species of people that believes in applying the scientific method to questions of baseball, I had another, secondary motive. I was hoping Bill James would prove to be even more insufferably pompous than I could have imagined.

The first thing I noticed about James was his Timex and his humdrum golf shirt tucked haphazardly into his pants. Nobody at the ballpark recognized him and, as far as I could tell, this didn't bother him one bit. In the van on the way to the game, James had answered all my turkeyball questions about statistics and baseball politely and carefully. As he talked, I'd been keyed in for a reference to himself in the third person or maybe an inflammatory comment about my teenage hero, Sparky Anderson.

So after a few minutes of hearing nothing like this, I asked a question I'd worked up on the drive down from New York—an anecdote involving Jason Giambi, Jose Guillen, and a bobbled ball in the outfield that was designed to challenge the very notion that accurate statistics can be kept on baseball, let alone be used to evaluate player performance. It was a trap I'd sprung to see if the "real" Bill James would emerge from his slumber, fangs exposed.

While he didn't spend much time trying to answer my ham-fisted question, he didn't take advantage of the opportunity to call me an idiot, either. Instead, he said this: "The world is vastly more complicated than anyone can understand. Therefore everyone has understandings of it, and only fools imagine that those understandings are so complete that they're immediately exclusive."

Bill James was, to my surprise, popping a pin in the notion that he had baseball figured out. The more I pushed, the more I realized he's actually a pundit in reverse: His goal is to tell people to beware of the opinionated, especially those people who preach any notion a little too ardently (even if that person's name is Bill James). For loyal Jamesian readers, this is elementary stuff. But at that point it was a revelation to me. I shut off the tape recorder.

As the game unfolded, James told a few funny stories about his new life in the front office of the Boston Red Sox, most of which revolved around how the team's brain trust (himself included) were just as baffled by the breakout performances of some of the team's players as the fans were. He wondered aloud if the modern benchmark for a closer these days should be 30 saves or 40, something he had no strong feelings about. He praised the accuracy of radar guns, talked about how the umpires were calling the traditional strike zone, and weighed in on an obscure rule that awards a batter a triple if a fielder throws his glove at the ball. The most animated I saw him was the moment he got his mitts on a beer.

Leaving the park after the game in Moyer's van, James broke a short silence by posing a question to the group. "Vada Pinson is the only Vada in major league history, and also the only Pinson," he said. The question was really a challenge to the group: identify all the players in baseball history who had two distinct names.

"Vida Blue?" I asked.

"There was another Blue," James said, "and there may be another Vida."

"How about Yorvit Torrealba?"

"There you go," James told me, before thinking better of it. "No, wait… there's another Torrealba. His brother…."

"Of course."

Steve Moyer piped up next. "Ichiro Suzuki, Akinori Otsuka and Kazuhito Tadano," he said, triumphantly.

"Bravo," someone said, and then everyone started throwing out names at once.

"Sixto Lezcano."

"Kirby Puckett!"
"Jolbert Cabrera."

***

It wasn't that Bill James had been thoroughly disarming that night, though he was. He'd been unassuming, too, which made it surprisingly hard for me to want to continue my lifelong *jihad* against him. In a few months, when the Red Sox won the World Series, I thought of the notion of Bill James getting a World Series ring and it made me genuinely happy. 'Good for Bill, he's earned it,' I thought.

What I realized on the long drive back to New York that night is that all this conversation about baseball was familiar to me. I'd heard it before—coming from my dad and his friends at dinner parties.

Thinking back, I probably shouldn't have been so surprised that Bill James had roped my dad. As a political science professor who came out of graduate school in the 1960s, Dad had been schooled under the old rules of academia where most people considered "political science" to be an oxymoron. Politics was personal, they believed, so it couldn't really be quantified by any means or understood by people who were outside the fishbowl.

No sooner had my dad settled in at the University of Michigan than his department was overrun by uppity kids who were intent on exposing this prehistoric view of politics as a pretty lazy and exclusionary way to think. At first, he resisted. But after a while he decided to drop his prejudice and have a look. The more he studied the data, the more he started to question the old assumptions he'd been taught and look for more empirical explanations. The moment he discovered that Bill James was doing the same thing in baseball, he was hooked.

To most kids, baseball is a game of movement. What's interesting to them is knowing when to break your wrists during a swing or how to approach second base on a steal attempt. It's a game of sights and sounds and superstitions and even smells—the mown grass, the sunbaked dirt, the scent of a newly oiled mitt.

What I couldn't understand as a teenager is that once your playing days are far behind you (as mine are), baseball splits in two. One half is the game that's played in the physical world, while the other exists solely in our minds. The further we venture from one of these two realms, the more we're inclined to ignore the other.

The truth was that baseball had changed: For me, and probably for a lot of kids from my generation, baseball wasn't really a game that could be shared by a father and son. To me, baseball was a game whose beauty lay in the feeling of hitting a ball in the fat part of the bat. To my dad, baseball was a game that was beautiful to reason with—beautiful in a way that a kid could not understand.

During my inaugural season in Tout Wars, I learned (often the hard way) that running any ballclub without paying heed to the latest advancements in analysis was an excellent way to get the crumbs knocked out of you. Before the season began, I swallowed my pride and hired a NASA mathematician to help me with the stats. Once I got over my reflexive distrust of all things numerical, I realized a lot of what Bill James was preaching was common sense. If anything, Bill James was responsible for a lot of kids who loved baseball (the way I once did) getting a chance to play in the majors—even if they didn't *look* like a ballplayer was supposed to. Maybe if James had been around a decade earlier, I could have been that lucky S.O.B. getting benched for Johnny Grubb.

Though Dad passed away before I had a chance to talk with him about baseball the way adults do, I haven't had to wonder what those conversations might be like. I just thumb through my new copy of the *New Historical Baseball Abstract* and I might as well be conducting a séance. So to Bill James, I'd like to officially forgive you for lobotomizing my dad, apologize to you for all my earlier venom (especially the nacho thing), and thank you for making baseball a hundred times more enjoyable for old farts the world over.

(Like me.)

When I first read Bill James' *Baseball Abstracts* in the early 1980s, they profoundly changed the way I looked at the game and even had an impact on my career. I was majoring in mathematics at a university in Massachusetts at the time but had not seriously considered the connection between my education and baseball. I had memorized the batting averages and ERAs of Major League players and had played simulated games for years, but baseball was not something that I had analyzed scientifically. James' writings led me to think more carefully about why teams won and lost games and to examine everything I thought I knew about baseball. He taught me to question traditional beliefs about batting orders, strategy, and player evaluation, and he showed me that the baseball establishment was not always correct. Baseball became more than just a leisurely pastime; it was now a sport that I spent as much time analyzing as watching.

Inspired by James, I started using baseball data in my classes at school and ultimately wrote a Master's thesis titled, "How to Win a Pennant in Major League Baseball." In my thesis, I used regression analysis to investigate the relationship between winning percentage and various other team statistics. Twenty years later, I am still analyzing the game on my blog and internet message boards and encouraging others to do the same. When I am not watching or studying baseball, I work as a research analyst in the behavioral health field and have never forgotten James' lesson about questioning everything that I think I know.

LEE PANAS
Research Analyst
Chelmsford, Massachusetts

When I was a kid, I collected baseball cards. From the front, I learned what my heroes looked like, but it was the back of the card that provided me with an education. For example, to this day I know that Fargo-Morehead is in North Dakota because when Roger Maris was in the minors he played there; I read it on the back of his baseball card.

But what I really learned was the fun of numbers. I was all about the Triple Crown. I figured out batting averages, ERAs, magic numbers. I'd even occasionally dabble in the esoteric slugging percentage. Throw in a few stolen bases, errors, hit-by-pitches, add the nicknames (Johnny Mize was "The Big Cat"), and I was set.

I read baseball books; I subscribed to *The Sporting News, Baseball Digest,* and waited for Street and Smith's *Baseball Annual* as if *Playboy* came out once a year. I talked baseball with my dad (who insisted that Mel Ott was the greatest player he ever saw), and I watched games on television and in person and listened to them on the radio, often twisting the dial so delicately in the hope of picking up a distant road game that I thought I had a future as a safe cracker.

Bottom line: I KNEW IT ALL! Guess again, Billy-Ball…it turns out you knew practically nothing. What I knew was the veneer, the façade that they wanted me to know, the information they let me know. It was enough for me, but it wasn't enough for Bill James. James cracked the Da Vinci code. No, I'm wrong, Bill James *is* Da Vinci. He created numerical formulas that validated (or disproved) the conventional wisdom that ruled baseball thinking then, and still tries to rule it now. Except Bill James won't let them.

BILL CHUCK
Writer
Brookline, Massachusetts

Slapping Myself on the Forehead

by Steve Moyer

President of Baseball Info Solutions

How did Bill James change my view of baseball? Well, let me tell you. The first time I attended a ballgame with him was a few years ago in Kansas City. Around the third inning, he said, "Steve, let me show you something. If you sit backwards in your seat, with your knees pointed toward the spectators behind you, then twist your head around and watch the game that way, all the secrets of sabermetrics will open up to you. It's kind of a Tantric thing." So I tried it, and ever since then, when I go to a ballgame, I sit that way. That's how Bill James changed my view of baseball.

***

OK, for real this time. The first time I remember paying attention to baseball was when, at seven years old, I decided I liked the Cardinals against the Red Sox in the 1967 World Series. (Ironically, when that Series replayed in 2005, I was rooting the other way.)

So there I was, a diehard Cardinal fan living in Eastern Pennsylvania. I liked the Cardinals because I couldn't possibly like the Phillies, Mets or Yankees like everyone else in the area (the contrarian in me started early).

I was pretty much the typical baseball fan: I thought all the players on my favorite team were the best players in the league. I distinctly remember insisting to my Phillie-fan friends that Cardinal third baseman Ken Reitz was a better player than Mike Schmidt because he hit for a higher batting average and had a better fielding percentage (true for the most part, in the early 1970s at least). If there was a Phillie player I did like as a child, it was Tony Taylor, their speedy, aggressive, scrappy, hustling little top-of-the-order second baseman.

Then Whitey Herzog took over in St. Louis and a friend of mine loaned me a new book called *The Bill James Baseball Abstract 1982.* I liked the book a lot, but I still didn't quite get the message, I guess. You see, I really liked Willie McGee, the Cards' speedy, aggressive, scrappy, hustling little top-of-the-order center fielder. And every spring, James would write stuff like this, from the *1984 Abstract,* in which McGee is ranked by James as the twentieth best center fielder in baseball at the time: "Showed some improvement. I still have no use for any of the Omar Moreno-type centerfielders."

Finally, in 1985, the Cardinals went to the World Series and Willie McGee won the MVP award. Bill James would now *have* to recognize how good McGee was, right? I imagined he would go on and on about how he'd underrated McGee in the past but had now come to his senses. Here's what I got instead, from the *1986 Abstract:* "Led N.L. in hitting both at home (.357) and on the road (.350), with 28 stolen bases each place but far more power on the road, up 21 extra base hits to 33.... Ranks fifth among active players in career batting average, .308."

This is the wording under James' description of McGee's ranking as the *second-best* center fielder in the National League, behind Dale Murphy!

SECOND? How could McGee not be even the best player at his position when he was the best player in the whole darn league? The sports writers even said so. Well, eventually, thanks to Bill James, I came to understand baseball things that I never knew before, things that a lot of folks in the baseball industry still don't understand today. I know now, for example, that good teams typically beat up on their opponents a lot, while one-run success often comes down to little more than chance. I know that speed is overrated. I know that pitching isn't "seventy-five percent of baseball" (thank goodness that phrase seems to have bitten the dust); that guys with low batting averages can be extremely valuable, if they do things like hit for power and walk; that those speedy, aggressive, scrappy, hustling little top-of-the-order players often aren't all the media and "baseball men" make them out to be—and that they often don't belong at the top of the order, either. (Actually, I've worked with people like this—guys who are always running here and there looking busy but seem to have a heckuva lot of trouble actually getting anything done. Business management overrates these guys just as much as baseball management does.)

About four or five months ago, I had never heard of OPS or Win Shares and didn't care if a player had an OBP of .400. Now, the first thing I look for is OBP and Win Shares, while I can care less if a player hits .300. And if he makes an out less than 60% of the time, he's awesome. I look at baseball in a totally different way now. Thanks, Bill!

TONY AUBRY
Student
Queens, New York

That's really how Bill James changed my view of baseball, turning me into a much more intelligent baseball fan. It's funny, between sabermetrics and fantasy baseball I've lost my love for one individual team. I no longer live and die by the St. Louis Cardinals or any other single franchise. These days, I root for my fantasy players, team clients of Baseball Info Solutions, and teams that seem to pay attention to sabermetrics. Some people would say it's terrible being a baseball orphan, but for me it's a lot better. My love of baseball is more pure now. I can see the forest for the trees. And I won't be telling you Ken Reitz was a better player than Mike Schmidt any time soon.

***

But the main thing I want to write about are my friend and colleague Bill James' great sense of originality and his readability. He has made a habit of "coming out of left field" (bad pun, I know) with his ideas. There's something in his brain that makes him constantly approach baseball and baseball history from an angle that hasn't occurred to the rest of us. In his early days, it was things as simple as pouring over box scores, doing his best to hand-figure the basic splits that are second nature to us today and to assign stolen bases and caught stealings to individual catchers and pitchers. Most recently it's been his Win Shares and Defensive Misplays/Good Plays.

Granted, Bill can crunch numbers with the best of them. There ain't many baseball stats that can match the complexity of Win Shares, for example. I know from experience that it takes a supersharp programmer literally weeks to wrestle the Win Shares system to the ground. But oftentimes, I'm more impressed with the simple, seemingly obvious nuances of baseball that Bill somehow realizes are important before the rest of the world gets there. Defensive Misplays/Good Plays are a perfect example.

As anyone who follows baseball closely knows, defensive errors are charged very sparingly. (Not to get off on a tangent, but as Craig Wright pointed out years ago in his excellent book *Diamond Appraised*, the assigning of errors is flawed too, being tremendously affected by home park, official scorer, etc.) On August 31, 2006, for example, in a play that's destined for blooper reels for years to come, Toronto Blue Jays outfielder Alex Rios, trying to catch a flyball off the bat of Red Sox utility infielder Alex Cora, accidentally swatted the ball with his bare hand over the fence and fifteen feet into the stands. Was this ruled an error? No, it was ruled a home run. Actually, it was Cora's first home run in many months. This play was an extreme example, of course, but there are plenty of times a defender should have or could have made a play yet doesn't get charged with an error. Bill was the first one to insist that we all admit this, begin to measure it, and then take it into account as we analyze individual players and teams.

On the flipside, Bill noticed that when a defender makes a good defensive play, he gets no more credit for such a play than for making a routine play. In the traditional scorebook, a leaping catch above the center field wall with the bases loaded looks the same as a "can of corn" pop-up—both are simply recorded "F8."

Bill decided it was time to document those things and categorize them. With the help of the Baseball Info Solutions labor pool, we now know, for example, that in 2006 Gary Matthews, Jr. was the best at reaching over the fence to steal a home run from hitters and that Jose Castillo ruined more potential double plays due to his bad throws than any other pivot man in baseball.

A key here is that when James told John Dewan and me about this idea, it made me want to slap myself on the forehead and say, "Why didn't I, as a passionate, sabermetrically-oriented baseball fan, think of that?"

Working in the baseball industry for fifteen years, I've seen more than my share of this: "Hey, let's add on-base percentage to at-bats and errors, then we'll divide that by plate appearances plus sacrifice flies and multiply the whole thing by .0264." Inevitably, the best players turn out to be Albert Pujols, A-Rod, or one of the other usual suspects. We need less of that kind of statistical analysis and more of the kind of simple originality Bill James continues to produce.

His originality of thinking also necessitates that his best literary work is produced when the least amount of format and procedure has to be followed. Next to the unbeatable *Bill James Historical Baseball Abstracts* (take your pick of the three versions for a crash course in baseball history—there's no better, more enjoyable place to start), the best Bill James reading lies in his underrated *Baseball Book* series, which ran from 1990-1992. These are, quite simply, 350-plus pages of whatever the heck Bill felt like writing about each year. The alphabetical "Biographical Encyclopedia" sections of these books—prose histories of player lives and careers, done in other historical books but of course not nearly as well—are fascinating. Like a mother bird, Bill was so good at chewing through baseball history and regurgitating it out in wonderfully digestible form. The fact that in three *Baseball Books* and over 150 pages of tiny print Bill didn't make it past the name "Baker" shows the thoroughness of his research and writing. If you can pick up a 1990s *Baseball Book* at a flea market or on eBay, the Harry Agganis, Dick Allen and Cap Anson bios alone will make whatever price you pay worth it.

All of this leads me to the unmatched readability of Bill's writing. As anxiously as I awaited the shipment of my new season Strat-O-Matic Baseball cards as a teen in the mid-1970s, each spring in the mid-1980s I anticipated the new *Abstract*. I'd start looking for the book in early February, even though I knew it wouldn't come out until March. (Yes, boys and girls, seasonal baseball publications actually arrived in March back in those days, not January, December, or even November like they do now. And to think, early on in my baseball industry days, we were told by book publishers that "baseball fans won't buy a baseball book until spring.") One year the *Abstract* didn't come out (at least in my area) until after the season had already begun, and it about drove me crazy.

Bill's writing has a tremendous personal feel, as if he's sitting next to you and telling you the story. If there's one thing that annoys me with baseball commentators, it's when they use "we" instead of "I," as in "we think the designated hitter rule is a great innovation." Who are the "we" those guys are talking about anyway? The writer and who else? Bill James and his co-authors never use "we" unless there truly is more than one person speaking. With Bill, it's always clear who is writing, and I like it that way.

Apparently, Bill didn't recognize the talent he had for readability. I've always wanted copies of his early self-published *Abstracts* and I've asked him about them. He tells me they're really not all that interesting anymore, that they are mostly filled with the kind of statistical analysis that is second nature to baseball fans these days. As for prose, he says there's not much, because it took him years to realize his audience actually enjoyed his meanderings. Bill kept most of that stuff to himself early on for fear of scaring customers away.

* * *

I'm a tough sell, but Bill James and his sense of humor gets me chuckling to myself. He wasn't afraid to be silly before silly invaded sports (and marketing in general) to the unbearable level it has today. How about these gems:

> Player comment from the *1983 Abstract:* "Tim Laudner—
> Name rhymes with 'Podner.'"

> Joe Orsulak comment from the *1987 Abstract:* "Did you
> ever notice that if you say Orsulak over and over it sounds
> like the noise you hear inside of a train? Another one of
> those is Quisenberry. If you say Quisenberry over and over
> and tap the table with a pencil when you hit the qs and bs it
> sounds like windshield wipers."

And there's always profound wisdom tucked away in his writings. My favorite comes from the *Baseball Managers* book. I actually
read this to the adult Sunday School class that I teach:

> Rube Foster was the greatest manager in the history
> of the Negro Leagues, not to mention a leading pitcher,
> the owner of the American Giants, and the de facto
> commissioner of Negro baseball. Foster usually had a pipe
> in his mouth, even when he was in the dugout, and like
> most pipe smokers, he wasn't going to take the thing out of
> his mouth to talk to you unless he actually had something
> to say. When he had a young player who didn't give quite
> the appropriate effort, Rube would take him aside and tell
> him this story:
>
> "A farmer had a donkey and an ox, which he worked as
> a team. It was hard work, and one day the ox decided just to
> stay in his stall all day and eat. When the donkey got back
> to the barn that night, the ox asked him, 'What did the boss
> say about me?'

"'Didn't say nothing,' said the donkey.

"The ox slept well that night, and when the farmer came out the next morning, the ox again balked at leaving the barn. When the donkey came back that night, he asked again, 'What did the boss say?'

"'Didn't say nothing,' the donkey answered, 'but he visited the butcher.'

"The next morning the ox was out of his stall early, waiting by the yoke when the farmer appeared.

"'You might as well go back to your stall,' the farmer told him. 'I've already sold you to the butcher.'"

So, I guess the moral of my little contribution to this book is this: "If you don't want to get sold to the butcher, read as much Bill James as you can get your hands on." Well, not exactly, but I would recommend reading as much Bill James as you can get your hands on anyway. Learning will never be more fun, especially the part about slapping yourself on the forehead.

I was ten years old in 1961, during the historic season in which Roger Maris hit 61 home runs and beat the revered home-run record of Babe Ruth. Even at the age of ten I was conscious of the constant abuse that Maris took from a statistically ignorant media and baseball establishment.

Although we can now appreciate, thanks to Bill James, the magnitude of Maris' accomplishments that season, the media could see nothing more than Maris' .269 batting average and vilified him daily. The manner in which he was treated both by baseball (the asterisk) and the media not only robbed Maris of the joys of his magnificent season but stayed with him throughout his career and even after his retirement.

I cannot help but think that had Bill James lived twenty years earlier and the fruits of his magnificent insights into the true nature of baseball statistics had existed in 1961, baseball history that season, and possibly Maris' life and career, would have been very different.

BOB TACHER
Attorney
Coral Springs, Florida

In my final days as a prosecuting attorney, I sent Bill James this in an email: "I keep seeing your interest in the literature of crime pop up in interviews. As a prosecutor, I wanted to make myself available for questions you might have about the criminal justice system."

Such *chutzpah* on my part. In his reply, which ran more than 2600 words, James advised me that he didn't want to have the judicial process explained to him, not by a lawyer. As he put it: "The usual input of lawyers into the public discussion of a crime case is … how do I put this? … not something that I value highly. The role of lawyers in discussing crime cases in public venues … is essentially identical to the role of athletes in the discussion of sports. Not to put too fine a point on it, they are essentially purveyors of bullshit."

It hadn't occurred to me until then that James' essays about baseball have been attacking the same stasis in the sport that keeps the justice system from functioning as well. Since then, he and I have exchanged tens of thousands of words about crime, including more than 15,000 words about the murder of JonBenet Ramsey. He understands that little girl's case better than anyone I know, and if he ever publishes a book about crime that includes his analysis of what actually happened, it'll go a long way towards removing all doubt about the innocence of the girl's mother, Patsy Ramsey. It will also drastically change how we all think about law and order in general.

James' and my Socratic dialogues have revolutionized the way I analyze my criminal cases as a defense attorney. Advice to young lawyers: To get ahead, read Bill James, not William Blackstone.

KEITH SCHERER
Attorney and Baseball Analyst
Chicago, Illinois

The Collision of Sabermetrics and Fantasy Baseball

by Ron Shandler

author of *Baseball Forecaster* and publisher of BaseballHQ.com

I have met Bill James only once in my life. This meeting occurred at a Society for American Baseball Research (SABR) convention in 1991. I was still working to find my place in the industry and had rented a table at the event to sell my *Baseball Forecaster*.

Bill James was browsing the exhibition hall and came upon my table. I greeted him and introduced myself; he whispered a coarse "hello" under his breath as he picked up one of my books. And then he stood there, silently thumbing back and forth through the book for at least two or three minutes. It felt like two or three hours.

During those "hours," I stood frozen, for here before me was my idol. It was his *1984 Baseball Abstract,* a casual summer purchase, that had effectively changed my life. As a baseball-stat geek by disposition and a statistical analyst by trade, I was completely taken in by his writing. James' *Baseball Abstract* opened the floodgates to an obsession that has lasted a lifetime. I spent the next few years devouring every baseball analysis publication I could get my hands on. I started trying to integrate my own pockets of expertise into the process. Eventually, it evolved into a new career.

***

I'm certain that Bill James did not know any of this as he stood there thumbing through my book. I hoped he saw me as someone who was trying to further the discussion that he had started. But it had been three years since his final edition of the *Abstract*, the one whose farewell essay revealed some underlying bitterness: "I used to write one 'Dear Jackass' letter a year," he wrote. "I now write maybe thirty.... I am encountering more and more of my own readers that I don't even like, nitwits who glom onto something superficial in the book and misunderstand its underlying message. I think that whenever a writer finds that he is beginning to dislike his own readers, it's a very clear sign that he's heading down the wrong road."

> Bill James helped rekindle interest in baseball for a generation of fans. He gave us a new way to look at the game, the players, and the statistics. Even those of us who don't have a scout's eye are able to evaluate players using his methods.
>
> **KEVIN CREMIN**
> Radio Producer/Engineer
> Seattle Mariners Radio Network
> Seattle, Washington

In retrospect, I am now at a point in my career when I can better understand where James was coming from then. Once you've done something for a long time, it becomes a personal challenge to have to prove yourself over and over again as new readers discover your work. But back in 1991, it was all still fresh and exciting, for me anyway.

After having spent those interminable minutes thumbing through my book, Bill James opened up to one page, leaned over the table to me, and pointed to a single number amidst an ocean of data. And he said, "This is wrong." Then, without another word, he closed the book, placed it back on the stack, and moved on to the next table.

After he was out of view, I reopened the book to the data point in question. It was the batting average of then Atlanta Braves prospect Andy Tomberlin. In those days of data entry by hand, I had mistyped Tomberlin's total at-bats; his batting average in the book *was* wrong.

***

There is no excuse for data errors, but I have always questioned the possibility of "precision" in a game played by human beings. Perhaps that is why I was equally drawn to another book I purchased that same summer. That book was called *Rotisserie League Baseball*. Bill James and his "sabermetrics" buddies provided insights into baseball, but not absolutes. Rotisserie or fantasy baseball thrived on the inherent uncertainty of what happens on the field. There was nothing precise about either. Still, both were founded on intelligent analysis; it was just that fantasy baseball was saddled with an unfortunate moniker: "fantasy," as in "unreal" or "fantastic" or "whimsical" or "illusionary." *The Lord of the Rings* was fantasy. Baseball was real to me, no matter what form it took.

My statistical analysis work, however, gravitated towards fantasy baseball because I saw more opportunities for me there. Bill James remained on his different course. I suppose he always will. We would never meet again. For a while, it looked like sabermetrics and fantasy might not either.

Michael Lewis, in his book *Moneyball*, writes that many of Bill James' readers were, in fact, fantasy baseball fanatics. This is true now, but it hasn't always been that way. Lewis attempts to tie the rise of fantasy baseball to James' success, but this line of thinking rings false to me.

For one thing, Lewis does note that it would be counter-intuitive for fantasy leaguers to find interest in James' work, since the Rotisserie game uses questionable evaluators of skill. But more than that, there was nothing in James' early work that spoke specifically to fantasy baseball. In fact, most 1980s fantasy leaguers I knew had little interest in the *Abstracts*; many never even heard of them. James, himself, was anything but a fan of Rotisserie, despite Lewis' assertions to the contrary: "James knew better than just about anyone on the planet just how many people were taking to these fantasy games...and, therefore, how deep the interest in baseball statistics. He became an investor and creative director of...STATS, Inc."

James may have joined STATS, Inc., but it likely had little to do with the fantasy industry. According to John Dewan, a founder and the former CEO of STATS, he asked James to develop his own fantasy game, using a set of rules that would better approximate the real game of baseball. The Bill James Fantasy Baseball game was a good game, but it was not what mainstream fantasy players were playing. In fact, James stayed as far away from the Rotisserie mainstream as possible. His few forays into the public roto world were not noteworthy.

For example, James participated in *USA Today Baseball Weekly's* debut League of Alternative Baseball Reality (LABR) experts league in 1994 and competed against such notables as Keith Olbermann, Rod Beaton, Alex Patton and me. James made just a handful of player moves all season, no trades, and finished in 11th place, 43 points out of 1st. He never competed in an experts league again.

The Bill James Player Ratings Book, published in 1993, 1994 and 1995, was clearly intended to capture the fantasy market. But if you read even just the introduction, you'll see an author who was still resisting the mainstream: "The players are evaluated on a dollar scale. The best player in baseball (Barry Bonds) is worth $100. Players who have retired or have been released and clearly aren't coming back have no value. Everybody else is somewhere between zero and $100.... There is no formula for these dollar values. They represent purely subjective judgments about the players. The values do not imitate any specific game except baseball. There are many "shadow games" that are based on baseball.... It's my assumption that many or most of you play those games, and bought this book to help you evaluate the players for your game."

Note that James always refers to fantasy leaguers in the second person; he never places himself among the members of the fraternity. Despite the fact that the Rotisserie "standard" at the time was a $260 budget and player values were precisely calculated, he opted to present a $100 limit with subjective player values. His disdain is further reflected in the following description of fantasy games, which appeared in the introduction to the 1993 edition but was excised from the subsequent two books: "The problem is that each of those games focuses on baseball through its own peculiar lens, and each one distorts the game in one way or another."

***

The fact that Bill James views fantasy baseball as a "distortion" is no surprise. It is an accurate characterization by someone who is, at his core, a baseball traditionalist. But what James did not see was that fantasy is a game unto itself, with its own unique links to the worlds of baseball and economics. War room strategists, for example, might look at the game of chess as a distortion of what they are interested in, but that takes nothing away from the unique allure of chess. In fact, insiders often refer to fantasy baseball as a six-month chess match.

James' resistance to fantasy, combined with his position as an industry leader, may have helped foster the philosophical wedge that exists between sabermetricians and fantasy leaguers. SABR, the organization from which the word "sabermetrics" was coined, boasts two dozen special interest groups—everything from Statistical Analysis to Music & Poetry—yet not one devoted to fantasy baseball. Serious analytical websites are loath to associate themselves in any way with fantasy baseball, unless it is to generate cash flow. Many fantasy leaguers view these groups as unnecessarily elitist.

I'll admit that fantasy baseball is anything but pure, but that does not make it bad. Fantasy games are not meant to be real baseball. They *are* "shadow games." In an era when home-team loyalty has been eroded by free agency and the real game's credibility has been tarnished by steroid scandals, fantasy baseball keeps fans connected to the game on the field. Baseball has to evolve to meet the needs of its changing fan base. The designated hitter, inter-league play, wild card teams, and fantasy baseball have all just been mileposts in the evolutionary process of keeping fans. Fantasy baseball cannot be dismissed as a mere distortion, even by someone as august as Bill James.

The truth is, "elitist" analysts and "distorting" fantasy leaguers not only can co-exist but can actually thrive when allowed to synergize. Michael Lewis was correct that fantasy leaguers eventually figured out that they needed some level of sabermetrics to win their games. Sabermetricians benefited, too, finding untapped pockets of expertise from within the huge fantasy marketplace. I myself have found fantasy leagues to be wonderful laboratories in which to test out sabermetric theories.

***

I often wonder what would have happened had Bill James fully embraced fantasy baseball and leveraged his work to support that growing marketplace. I believe the impact would have been tremendous. For one, the explosion in interest in baseball analytics might have occurred as much as a decade earlier. For good or bad, fantasy leaguers are a huge market force that could have driven this interest.

Another change might have been in professional baseball itself. Fantasy baseball is still viewed through a jaundiced eye by Major League Baseball. Unlike the National Football League, which has created a partnership with their fantasy industry, Major League Baseball sees fantasy as a revenue stream to control, and the individual ballclubs continue to maintain their distance. Had fantasy been more closely linked to sabermetrics from the beginning, thus legitimizing it, we might be seeing more teams doing things like what the San Francisco Giants did in 2006—provide a paid internship to a fantasy league winner.

Finally, had Bill James recognized fantasy baseball for the intellectual pursuit that it is, he would probably own the industry right now. All of us self-proclaimed fantasy gurus would now be working for him.

What an incredible Think Tank might have emerged from that.

I t was a beautiful summer day, June of 1979. I walked over to my friend Phil Meade's home to play our favorite table top baseball game, Strat-O-Matic. Before we sat down to play, Phil said, "Hey Tommy, did you see this?" He proceeded to let me read his copy of the third edition of Bill James' self-published *Baseball Abstract*. It had month-by-month batting records, an analysis of Jim Rice versus Ron Guidry for the 1978 MVP, account-form box scores, and analysis of each team.

Most importantly, it said my Red Sox had great pitching and defense but a mediocre offense. But, James said, all this was masked by their playing half their games in Fenway Park, a hitter's paradise. Since this was exactly what I thought about the Sox, I immediately wrote down the address, a post office box in Kansas City, and mailed off a check for $6. Soon after, my own *Abstract* arrived in the mail. I have been reading Bill James ever since. What I like about him is that he writes in a clear, concise form about something complicated and makes it easily understood. He has the ability to see things others cannot.

TOM NAHIGIAN
Office Administrator
Los Angeles, California

We used to laugh at Eddie "The Walking Man" Yost when I was a kid. Yost was the "Good Field, No Hit" third baseman for the Washington Senators of the 1950s. Yes, THOSE Washington Senators—the ones made infamous back in the day by the slogan, "Washington: First in war, first in peace, and last in the American League."

Eddie Yost was the thick-handled-bat-using lead-off man for some of the worst teams of all time. He never hit .300, struggled to hit more than 9 HRs a year, and had no speed. A bum, right? We laughed at him: "Hey Yost, go back to little league, you Punch-and-Judy hitter!"

Why did we laugh at Eddie Yost? Because all that we kids knew were the stats we saw on the back of our baseball cards. Yost: 1956 avg: .231, HR: 11, RBI: 53, R: 94 (wait a minute, how many runs?), Ks: 82, BB: 151 (wait a minute, how many walks?).

If only fans had had Bill James back then. If only general managers had had Bill James back then. Heck, if only Eddie Yost's agent had had Bill James back then. (Really, if only Eddie Yost had HAD an agent back then.) Eddie Yost might have been a star. Bill James would have explained to us that Eddie "Good Field, No Hit" Yost was not a bum. He would have pointed out that Eddie "The Walking Man" Yost led the league with those 151 walks and that Eddie "Punch-and-Judy" Yost had an on-base percentage of .412—good enough for sixth best in the AL, even with his anemic batting average. And Bill James would have pointed out that those 94 runs were eighth best in the league, even though the seventh place Senators finished next to last in the league in runs scored.

There are a thousand Eddie Yosts in baseball's record books and on the field today. It took one man, Bill James, to hand us the keys to unlock their true value.

MIKE "MURPH" MURPHY
Host, The Mike Murphy Show,
WSCR "The Score" 670 Radio
Chicago, Illinois

Baseball, Basketball, Whatever

by Daryl Morey

Assistant General Manager of the Houston Rockets

Bill James taught me early on the dangers of assigning much value to randomness—in baseball or in life. In my present position as the GM-to-be of an NBA team, the Houston Rockets, I find this advice extremely relevant each day as I head into work. Yet, James is at the center of several serendipitous events that have led to my current position, and I am not sure how things would have ended up for me otherwise. I am constantly humbled by these events and respectful of the many people who are very talented yet have never received so much as the proverbial "cup of coffee" in their efforts to follow their dream of playing or working in sports.

***

My interest in James' ideas began with reading the *Baseball Abstracts* while growing up a Cleveland Indians fan in small town Ohio. Besides the pure enjoyment the *Abstracts* provided me, I learned that beliefs—whether they were about sports or any other endeavor in life—should always be examined. When I left school for college at Northwestern University in Evanston, Illinois, the *Abstracts* were one of the few things I packed in my overloaded small car.

Early in my freshman year at Northwestern, I learned that STATS, Inc. was in a suburb of Chicago only one town over from Evanston. One extremely nervous interview later I had a position helping to operate their Bill James Fantasy Baseball game. STATS was a small company and very open to allowing me to help in any area of the business where I could add value, including doing some work on modifying James' "Pythagorean Expected Wins" approach to other sports, such as basketball. My work at STATS also caused me to focus my university studies on statistics.

After college I went to work for The Parthenon Group, which happened to be advising a group attempting to purchase the Red Sox. While that group ultimately did not buy the team, the work on that case was noticed by Steve Pagliuca of Bain Capital. He referred us to Wyc Grousbeck, who happened to be considering a purchase of the Celtics at the time. We advised Wyc on the purchase, and he eventually became the principal owner of the team. Working with Wyc and eventually Danny Ainge was a once-in-a-lifetime opportunity. Both were amazingly open to trying new approaches to gain a competitive edge wherever we could find one. It was their willingness to invest in research that allowed us to advance the state of basketball analysis, and this was what caught the eye of Leslie Alexander at the Rockets, who offered me my present job.

What has the research in basketball found so far? While I cannot share the state-of-the-art information of what we are working on (we do want to maintain that competitive edge, you know), I can share a few basic principles that Bill James (and others) advocate in baseball that apply to basketball…and a few that do not apply.

***

The first principle is: Past performance is the best predictor of future success. I think this principle works throughout life, not just the sports industry. If someone cannot succeed on a lower level, it seems difficult to understand why he or she would start to succeed at the next higher level. Amazingly, this principle continues to be ignored by the leadership of multiple teams in multiple sports (not to mention politics, business, education, and even religion). Sports are littered with examples of players (such as Darko Milicic, selected in the draft ahead of Carmelo Anthony and Dwayne Wade) with limited records of success that decision-makers hope will succeed at the next level due to their athleticism, physical attributes, "intangibles," etc.

This "past performance" principle, however, is a necessary but not sufficient condition to succeed. While it is almost universally true that someone who has not succeeded at a lower level will most likely fail at a higher level, the odds are still very long that someone who succeeds at a lower level will succeed at the professional level, especially when it comes to a high-performance job like professional athlete (or professional athletic manager, for that matter).

I could give you a long list of people who have failed in the "majors," despite having succeeded in the minors, but hey, I'd like to keep at least some of my friends. Besides, I'm just starting my first stint in the buck-stops-here seat, so who am I to throw stones? All I'm saying is that Bill James is right: Past performance is the best predictor of future success. But it is not a slam dunk!

Another principle is: "It has always been done that way" is not a good reason to do anything. While respect and understanding must be paid to history, tradition, and past success, often the conditions and assumptions that made a process or decision correct in the past are no longer true, yet the assumptions often have not been examined in some time. For example, in baseball the dogma of playing for one run (by bunting, stealing, etc.) came about generally when the level of scoring was much lower than it is today. In football, there continues to be prescribed "rules" on when to "go for it" versus kicking a field goal on fourth down (such as fourth and goal from the two-yard line) that overwhelmingly have been shown to be sub-optimal decisions in almost all circumstances, but the mistake continues to be repeated. In basketball, despite the fact that manipulating the clock to get the last shot of a quarter (commonly known as going for the two-for-one) has been proven to be the best play in most circumstances, there are still many teams that do not attempt it.

As I start my career as a basketball general manager, I have no intention of throwing out the baby with the bathwater. A lot of guys who are a lot smarter than I am have done a lot of things right in the past. I plan to learn from them and build on what they have done. However, I will always remember what Bill James taught me: If I can't think of a better reason for my decisions other than the fact that it is the way it has always been done, then I'm probably not going to be around for very long.

***

I will highlight two principles that I don't think cut it in basketball. First is: Make the playoffs and you have a good shot at winning the whole thing. Actually, this is not a Bill James principle at all, although I think he would agree with it (especially after the White and Red Sox won back-to-back World Series Championships and the Cardinals won it all after winning only 83 games in the regular season). This principle is generally true in baseball and football, as low-seeded playoff teams often do win the title. In football it is because each game is one-and-done, which introduces the statistical possibility of a mediocre team having the game of its life while a great team goes into a temporary funk. In baseball it is because the intrinsic advantage that a better team has over a lesser team is much smaller. Remember, the worst team in baseball still wins about a third of its games, and the best team loses about a third. In basketball, however, a seven-game series each round and the large win-percentage advantage the top teams have over the lesser teams make it nearly impossible to win a title without being one of the top four to six teams in the regular season. The few exceptions to this rule (including the 1994-95 Rockets team, which won only 47 of its regular season games) are primarily because their regular season performance is not indicative of their intrinsic strength. In the 1994-95 Rockets case, regular season injuries and a significant late season trade for Clyde Drexler dramatically changed the face of the team in the playoffs.

This difference between basketball and other sports leads to different conclusions on how much appetite for risk a team should have when they make personnel decisions. Generally, the willingness to take risk should be high in basketball relative to baseball and football. This is because a team needs to be one of the top teams to win and a team cannot win without elite players. A strategy of managing your roster to simply make the playoffs each year and hoping for the best even if you are not one of the top teams does not work. This is why you often see more chances taken at the top of the NBA draft on very young high school players.

The second principle that does not cut it in basketball relative to baseball is that a player's value is similar no matter what team he is on. For example, in baseball the impact of Albert Pujols being swapped for a replacement level outfielder on the Kansas City Royals might take the Royals from 60 to 68 wins in a year, and his impact on the Yankees might take them from 100 to 108 wins. Eight extra wins in both cases. In basketball this is not true. Style of play has a much larger impact on the value of a particular player to a particular team, and the value can be non-linear. For example, a strong offensive rebounder (such as Jeff Foster) will have a larger impact on a team that currently wins more through defense and misses more shots on the offensive end (such as the current Pacers) than he would on a team with a high shooting percentage but poor defense. In our current Rockets situation, a player like Shane Battier who is a highly efficient scorer even though he does not take many shots is more valuable when you have an efficient primary volume scorer such as Yao Ming. Shane would not be as much help to a team without a primary scorer, because he is not someone who can create his own offense.

***

Bill James changed not only how I view the game of baseball but also how I view the game of basketball. More importantly to me, however, is that he has changed my view of life in general. Plus he helped prepare me for a really cool job. Thanks, Bill.

first learned about baseball by memorizing the backs of my 1955 Topps cards, listening to the Cardinals on KMOX in St. Louis, and filling up reams of notebook paper with scoresheets from Cadaco-Ellis All Star Baseball games I played. When I got older, I discovered Bill James' work and was hooked immediately. But it was never the numbers alone that attracted me to his writings. His *Bill James Historical Baseball Abstract* is arguably the best book ever written about baseball. In his annual *Baseball Abstracts*, time and time again he skewered common baseball wisdom, questioned longstanding assumptions, and generally had a hell of a good time doing it. But, James being James, he always had the numbers to back up his argument.

It was his voice, his perspective, his knack for uncovering just the right anecdote, his radical insights into the game of baseball, his passion for the Kansas City Royals and dislike of Steve Garvey, that made me appreciate the greatness of his work. Above all, it was his love—at times a tough love—for the game of baseball and its history, personalities, legends and myths. I believe that Bill James will one day be enshrined in Cooperstown for his many contributions to the great American game.

DENIS TELGEMEIER
Writer
Pleasanton, California

Ready for the Next Question

by Susan McCarthy

artist, graduate student, and wife of Bill James

To be perfectly honest, Bill James has not only influenced the way I view baseball, he's my filter to almost everything about the game. You see, he dragged me into baseball in the first place. How was I to know what a huge place baseball would have in my life when I first met Bill? Now, having been married to him for almost three decades, I've learned that everything eventually leads back to baseball.

I grew up in a family of medium-tempered sports fans. Following sports had its place in my family, but no one was out of control. Dad favored college football and basketball, wrestling, boxing and the Olympics. Mom paid some attention to whatever everyone else was interested in, but baseball was hers. She's more a radio listener than a TV watcher, and baseball games on the radio fit nicely into her life of multi-tasking to the demands of five kids and a husband.

As I was growing up, I didn't really like or dislike the game of baseball. But I must admit I had strong negative associations with Major League Baseball, mostly because of Sunday afternoons. That was my least favorite day of the week. During the school year, Sundays meant doing homework, ironing the gym suit (which reminded me of the one class I dreaded above all others), staying home because stores were closed, and hearing baseball on the radio. On those long boring Sunday afternoons, my mom was usually typing something for my dad on a manual typewriter while half-listening to the Royals game. This meant she wasn't as available to answer the demands of the kids, which in turn usually meant chaos among the rank and file.

***

Prior to my reading Bill James for the first time, if you would have told me that a .300 hitter with 100 RBI could be an inferior baseball player, my reply would have suggested that you seek serious medical attention. Thanks to enlightenment that James has provided through his writing, I now realize that everything in terms of baseball performance results should be examined in context rather than accepted at face value. For me, Bill James sent hardball conventional wisdom to the elephant graveyard.

STEVE LOMBARDI
Human Resources Manager
Monmouth County, New Jersey

So that's a little of my background before I met Bill at a Stokely Van Camps bean factory in the summer of 1975. We'd only talked a few times, but I remember standing in the hallway outside the women's locker room telling Bill I was going to a Royals game with my family that weekend. I had no idea then that he was a baseball fan, but in retrospect I realize the significance of the exchange. I can still see the look he gave me; he definitely raised his eyebrows. As I got to know him better, it became clear that he liked baseball. What didn't become apparent to me until I'd known him about a year was the extent of his obsession. It's not as if he hid it from me; it's more that he just didn't display the obsession openly. Baseball kept popping up in our conversations. When I visited his apartment, I noticed the *Baseball Encyclopedia* was always close by. Then I noticed the stacks of *The Sporting News*. But the most curious thing to me was the spiral notebooks filled with page after page of columns of numbers. It didn't really look like research. It looked more like something you'd do to keep your mind occupied. I honestly didn't know quite what to make of it.

Like any young couple there were many things we enjoyed doing together—going to movies, taking walks, listening to music, talking about books. What gradually became more obvious to me, though, was that Bill's mind was almost always on baseball. Unless there was a distraction. I could be very moody and sometimes if I seemed distant he must have thought he'd better start paying more attention to me. He would say, "A penny for your thoughts?" That was a hard question for me to answer because my mind could be anywhere. I never had to play that game with him though. I came to understand, if we weren't talking about something else, his mind was on baseball. It's just that simple.

You might be wondering how our relationship thrived—a neophyte paired with an obsessive-compulsive. Looking back on those early years, it's almost as if Bill drew me into the game when I wasn't watching. He didn't try to recruit me; he didn't make demands; he didn't have expectations. What he did was start teaching me about the game by letting me drive the discussion. I became more and more curious about what captivated him. I asked lots of questions—very basic, elementary questions. But he didn't seem to care what I knew or if I had forgotten what he already taught me. Bill still says that I didn't even know who Willie Mays was when I first knew him. That may be true, but if it is I know he would never have reacted by exclaiming, "You don't know who WILLIE MAYS is? Why he's…." Bill didn't seem to be judgmental, at least toward me.

We would take long walks in those early days. During the baseball season he would slip a small transistor radio in his front shirt pocket so he could periodically check on the Royals' game while we walked. Usually we'd just walk around Lawrence, Kansas, but on three occasions we took day walks of about twenty miles each. From Lawrence to a small town nearby named Eudora, we walked along country roads, and I distinctly remember Bill explaining his idea about the defensive spectrum. It seemed so obvious and basic that I was surprised it wasn't common knowledge. When we arrived in Eudora, we found a little small town café where we rested our legs and ate a soft-serve ice cream cone. I don't remember the walk back, but that evening we watched.... (OK, at this point my memory fails me, so I ask Bill, "Hey, remember that walk we took to Eudora?"

"Yeah," he says.

"Well, I know we watched a game that night but I can't remember anything about it."

Bill doesn't hesitate and says it was a World Series game and Tommy John was pitching. He reaches for one of the encyclopedias near his desk and finds the game. October 14, 1977. Oh, and he says we talked about Tommy John on the way back from Eudora.)

***

Since I knew almost nothing about baseball, my mind was like a blank page. (But I'm admitting to a blank page on that subject only. Well, OK, that, and golf, and maybe the fundamentals of mechanics.) One time, shortly after we were married in November of 1978, we tried a joint teaching project. I wanted to teach Bill to play the piano better; he wanted to teach me the basic standards of excellence in baseball. The piano lessons did not go well, and since he gave up on my lessons, I wouldn't sit for his either. But I still remember those standards. In retrospect I think if his approach had been to "educate" me by starting with basics and then proceeding with more advanced concepts, he probably would have scuttled my interest a long time ago. Instead he followed where my interest took us. I probably understood the runs created formula before I had mastered the whole right/left orientation. But the point is that even knowing how spotty my knowledge was, Bill talked to me about whatever he was working on. So what if I didn't know how to figure ERA? That didn't prevent him from explaining his theory of Defensive Efficiency (DER). The way he teaches is the way he writes. He makes a complex concept accessible, even to an ignoramus.

In the mid-late 1970s our hometown team, the K.C. Royals, was a well-run organization and one of the best teams in the majors. Learning about baseball by following the Royals probably helped draw me into the game too. Bill respected Ewing Kauffman greatly and would try to explain why he was a good owner. Since he grew up following the K.C. A's, I heard many stories about former owner Charlie Finley and comparisons between the two organizations. Kauffman had the idea for the Royals Academy, which selected athletes with tremendous raw ability but not great baseball skills. Bill respected this innovation. Frank White, for one, came out of that system. He also loved Royals player Amos Otis. Otis may have been the first player I remember Bill heralding as "his" kind of player. Not flashy, not widely touted, but a good percentage player. As a fan now, I also like to pick as favorites not those who are most widely regarded but players who are different for some reason.

Speaking of favorites, most everyone loved and admired George Brett in the 1970s and 1980s. Bill impressed upon me what a privilege it was to have a player of his caliber on our team. Those discussions would lead to talk about the Hall of Fame and about which players were the most likely to get in. Bill has worked on multiple systems to analyze this question, and it seems as if he was always tinkering with different approaches to the problem. Oftentimes I think he would try to work a problem through by talking about it. Bill's theories about aging players were always particularly interesting to me. Watching a game with him, I'd have to know how old a player was. He usually not only knew the age but the player's birth date. Or I'd want to know where he grew up; did he come from the farm system or a trade? Kinda spoils you after a while—no need to exert yourself and find a reference book; just ask Bill. Made me a very lazy fan.

Bill always wanted more data, and to this end he developed ways of scoring a game pitch by pitch. I don't think he was the first to score games with these added details, but he had his own system. The pitch-by-pitch accounts soon gave way to scoring where each ball was hit. I had to learn these rigorous methods just in case he had to go to the bathroom during a game. As a novice scorer, I admit I had to run through all the defensive positions consecutively before coming up with the right position number. Eventually I came to enjoy scoring a game, but that pitch-by-pitch stuff was too intense for me. It didn't give me a chance to relax and spy on the couple two rows ahead of us, for one thing. But by scoring a game, I found I could at least remember some of the highlights as we walked back to the car, though my mind is not anything like the mental filing system for baseball details Bill uses.

During the *Baseball Abstract* years, Bill generated many stats by pouring over *The Sporting News* or the *Baseball Encyclopedia*. As a world class procrastinator, he was also always behind in meeting a book deadline, mostly because he had so many more studies to include than he had time to get done. With a mid-December deadline for the *Abstract,* I remember how frustrated I would be thinking the "book crunch" was winding down, only to discover Bill had just started a new study. I typed large portions of the manuscripts in the early days and later on entered data into the computer. Sometimes I would help out by doing some of the

> **B**ecause of Bill James I quit being an actuary and now consult with sports organizations, including the Major League Baseball Players Association, the Strat-O-Matic Game Company, sports agents and other cool clients. What could be better than that?
>
> **BOB MEYERHOFF**
> Consultant
> Deerfield, Illinois

research. In 1981, I counted stolen bases against catchers by going through issues of *The Sporting News* and then going back over the box scores time and time again trying to find my errors. It was frustrating, but the next season I knew a lot more about catchers.

***

There are few more momentous occasions in one's life than the birth of a child. March 29, 1986, was such a date for Bill and me as we welcomed Rachel McCarthy James into the world. Our alma mater, Kansas University, was playing Duke in the semi-finals of the NCAA Basketball Championship later that afternoon. It hardly seemed to matter to us when KU lost; we had a healthy little girl and everything was all right in our world. That evening Bill and I were trying our best to digest the special new parents' meal, which was absolutely the worst steak dinner I've ever had in my life (sorry Jefferson County

North Hospital). Bill was seated on a chair next to my bed, telling me the story of the 1919 Black Sox scandal. I can't remember how the topic came up, but exhausted though I was, I found the story fascinating. We must have talked for several hours. Remembering this episode years later, I've thought, shouldn't we have been talking about how perfectly wonderful our little girl was and basking in the glow of the moment? No. Big event or little incident, it's always a good time for a baseball story if you live with Bill James.

I wondered how Bill would be with our three kids. Would he try to interest them in baseball? Would he be disappointed if they didn't love and enjoy his game? Would he get hung up hoping one or both of his two sons, Isaac and Reuben, had athletic ability and could be a baseball player?

Bill certainly has encouraged our kids' interest, but in an even-handed way. For instance, Bill insisted that I not count the time watching baseball as "screen time." (I agreed as long as they weren't flipping back and forth between other shows.) He was always ready to play catch with any of them, and this became one of Isaac's favorite things to do with his dad. When we attended games in K.C., Bill passed out packs of baseball cards to everyone to generate a little discussion during the hour-long drive. Sometimes it worked; other times we just read or looked out the window, wishing card packets still included gum. Between the ages of about eight and fourteen, Rachel routinely brought a book or two to any baseball game. She would read through the whole game, only to perk up when it was time for her fifth-inning cotton candy. Bill never asked her to stop reading and pay attention to the game. I remember a couple times he tried to interest Isaac in scoring. It didn't really take and Bill let it go. Reuben always liked the stuff of baseball and Bill would happily miss a few innings to take him to the souvenir shop.

Long ago I figured out that if I wanted to know this man, I needed to learn about baseball. Baseball still drives his life and occupies his mind. For me, baseball is a game I love and enjoy, but it is not my passion. Over the years my interest in the game has faded in and out. Before kids, I listened to the Royals game almost every night while working in my studio. Now, with three children and a busy life, I don't do that regularly anymore. (But unlike when I was a teenager, I love listening to games on the radio.) Our kids are all baseball fans, but their interest waxes and wanes too. Sometimes they will ask their dad lots of questions about the Red Sox; other times they don't seem to be paying much attention to what's happening in the season. If Bill notices, it doesn't seem to bother him. We know he doesn't hold it against us if we're not up to his level. He just wants us to enjoy the game however we choose. While we know he's *always* ready for our next question.

The Bill James Way of Life

by Rob Neyer

ESPN analyst and author of *The Big Book of Baseball Blunders*

I win.

Don't get me wrong; I know this book is not a contest.

If it *were* a contest, though? I would win. I'd lap the field twice; I'd have a six-touchdown lead at halftime; I'd throw a perfect game and hit two grand slams. Because Bill James changed not only my brain chemistry and the way I think about baseball and just about everything else, but also my life. My family thinks I'm famous, which of course is ridiculous. George "Batman" Clooney is famous; Michael "Moneyball" Lewis is semi-famous; and Rob "No Nickname" Neyer is a negligible footnote in the annals of sports "journalism." Nevertheless, I've been lucky enough to make a good living, write a few books that have met with favorable notices, and get my mug on TV every so often. Without Bill James none of it would have happened.

I don't know what my parents thought about me when I dropped out of college when I was almost twenty-two, but any objective outside observer would have wondered what the hell I was doing with my life. I certainly didn't know.

Then Bill James came along.

***

It was November 13, 1988. I know the date because I still have the letter I wrote to Bill James after Mike Kopf told me that James planned to hire a research assistant. I had an edge: I lived in Lawrence, Kansas, and James lived in Winchester, only twenty-five miles away. Still, I was mildly surprised when he asked me to meet him for an interview. I was wildly shocked when he called a few weeks later and said, "I'd like to hire you to work for me."

You have to understand: If you had asked me, at any particular moment over the previous four years—since shortly after I first picked up one of his books in the fall of 1984—which job I would have if I could have any job in the world, "working for Bill James" would have been my answer without a second's reflection. I offer that piece of information not as an excuse so much as an explanation for my bit of dishonesty in the interview. James asked me to provide a transcript from my four years at the University of Kansas—James went to KU too, by the way (another edge for me?)—and I told him I couldn't at the moment because I'd lost a library book. The truth? My four years in school included two good semesters, one decent one, and a whole lot of nothin'. If James had seen my transcript, he wouldn't have hired me. Or so I thought. I didn't intend to find out, and James never did press me on the matter. (Thanks for that too, Bill!)

I spent exactly four years as Bill James' full-time research assistant, which to this day remains some sort of record. Since then, Bill and I have kept in touch, and we wrote a book together. As I consider those four years today, I wish I'd been a better worker and I wish I'd been a better learner. I never forgot how lucky I was, but it was too easy to forget the preciousness of each day. I didn't take full advantage of a wonderful opportunity...but then, how many of us do? We learn what we learn, and some of what we learn sticks with us and makes us a bit smarter the next time around.

What have I learned from Bill? Well, it's almost literally true that everything I ever needed to know about baseball I learned from Bill James. And it's also true that much of what I know about everything else I learned from Bill James.

***

Example: writing. When I applied for the job with Bill, he asked me to provide a writing sample. I think I might have weaseled my way out of that one too, but if I did give him anything it would have been a paper I'd written for a class three or four years earlier. That is, if there was any evidence at all that I could write it was based on whatever skills I'd brought with me from high school. By the standards of high school, I was pretty good. But I didn't consider becoming a *writer*: I never wrote for the school newspaper, didn't join the yearbook staff, never wrote a poem or a short story for the literary journal.

Nevertheless, Bill hired me, and within a few months he was asking me to write drafts of articles for his next book. I suppose he simply growled to himself for a while upon reading the initial results, but eventually I arrived at the office one morning and found on my desk a long critique of my writing. I meant to save that memo, and it might still be somewhere in my house, nestled within a stack of papers I should have pitched into the recycling bin years ago. But I have not forgotten Bill's salient criticisms. For example, I'd said of some player—Billy Almon, I think—that at one point he "was released."

No, no, no! (Bill wrote.) *He was not released. He EARNED his release. Things do not happen to people. People DO things.*

> **L**ove him or hate him, agree or
> disagree, you cannot argue
> the profound impact Bill
> James has had on the way athletic
> performance is viewed. Now all
> we need is a stat to figure out why
> that is.
>
> **PATRICK LAGREID**
> Book Reviewer
> Seattle, Washington

As I read that, and re-read it, and re-read it again—this sort of thing went on for some pages, by the way, and I've omitted the curse words—I took Bill's vehement editorial comments as *editorial* comments; that is, tips about writing. But though I didn't realize it then, the real lesson was about more than writing; it was about living. Bill would not suggest, nor would I, that things don't happen to people. If you're walking along minding your business and a cement truck turns you into a man-sized pancake, it happened *to* you. But let's not kid ourselves; most of what happens to us is of our own making.

That's one of the lessons I learned from Bill James. For another, let's turn to science writer K.C. Cole, who once wrote, "In science, feeling confused is essential to progress. An unwillingness to feel lost, in fact, can stop creativity dead in its tracks." Bill has never been unwilling to feel lost. Actually, nearly all of us feel lost occasionally; what distinguishes Bill, I think, is that he's not afraid to admit it. For many years, he was known for (among many other things) his dislike of so-called "one-run strategies," particularly the sacrifice bunt. After all, if Earl Weaver didn't like to bunt, why should anybody else? In the back of Bill's mind, though, he must have known he didn't *know* enough about bunts to write about them with any authority. In the parlance of Donald Rumsfeld, what Bill had was a "known unknown," and it bothered him. So a dozen or so years after Bill became famous—a point at which he could easily have coasted on his previous work—he did the work and discovered that the true story about bunting wasn't nearly as simple as he'd once suspected. He didn't come down on one side or the other; rather, he simply said, "Umm, guys? Let's think about this some more. Because just in this little study I've done, it looks like there's a lot more going on than we thought."

That took courage, because the moment you admit that you might have been wrong about something the nattering nabobs will seize upon your uncertainty and attempt to weaponize it, which is all the easier because they probably didn't bother trying to understand what you had meant in the first place.

Another of these: A few years ago Bill wrote an article, "Underestimating the Fog," for the Society for American Baseball Research (SABR) that made a big splash, even getting into *The New York Times* (perhaps an all-time first for an article in a SABR journal). The first paragraph was funny (and I hope somebody else in this book illustrates how funny Bill can be). The second paragraph was startling:

> I have come to realize, over the last three years, that a wide range of conclusions in sabermetrics may be unfounded, due to the reliance on a commonly accepted method which *seems*, intuitively, that it ought to work, but which in practice may not actually work at all. The problem has to do with distinguishing between transient and persistent phenomena, so let me start there.

When Bill James, certainly the most famous and influential sabermetrician, writes of "conclusions in sabermetrics," he is of course writing to some large degree about himself. He is saying, essentially, "You know all that stuff you've been reading in my books for the last twenty-five years? I might have been wrong about a lot of it."

Much of the reaction to "Underestimating the Fog" was, well, reactionary. Much of it was thoughtful. But without getting at the question of whether Bill was fundamentally right or wrong—and you can read the article on the Web if you're interested—the point here is that Bill, well into his career and well past the point at which his fans demand it of him, still is not only willing but apparently eager to question everything he's done.

And he always has been. I recently read the entire run of *The Bill James Baseball Abstract Newsletter*, which was published for a couple of years in the middle 1980s, and ran across this passage:

> It isn't *numbers* that makes sabermetrics. It is not the use of *formulas* which creates knowledge. It is the search for the truth. A sportswriter starts with the conclusion, looks at the facts and selects those which fit the conclusion. A sabermetrician starts with the issue, looks at the facts and attempts to find the conclusion which fits the facts. All of the facts. There is nothing wrong with what the sportswriter does, but the goal of sportswriting "analysis" is to *convince*, and the goal of sabermetrics is to *learn*.

The Bill James Way of Life—and by the way, he would never in a million years come up with a label like that—is not easy. It certainly allows for complexity and inscrutability, but also demands a good-faith effort to find answers. If you read Bill's words and you buy into them, I mean *really* buy into them, you have to believe that our successes involve a fair amount of luck and our failures involve...well, sure, a fair amount of luck. But a fair amount of *our* failure too. If you buy into Bill James, you also have to believe that the easy answer often isn't the right answer and that finding the right answer might well involve a fair amount of work. And even when you think you've arrived at the right answer, you must always carry, in the back of your mind, the distinct possibility that you really weren't so right after all. That's not easy. Another thing that's not easy: Bill James can turn one into a crashing skeptic, unwilling to believe much of *anything* that doesn't come with a healthy dollop of evidence. Which means a Jamesian is often put in the uncomfortable position of either smiling and nodding uncomfortably or asking uncomfortably skeptical questions.

Not that you've got much of a choice. Bill James either changes your life or he doesn't. On this particular question, personally, I think I've come up with the right answer. But I could be wrong.

Bill James Is Worth the Wait

by John Dewan

owner of Baseball Info Solutions and co-publisher of ACTA Sports

I put the book down and stared into space. I had just read an article that Bill James wrote in his *1984 Baseball Abstract,* and I was mesmerized.

James was describing a grassroots project he was proposing. It was almost exactly one that I had dreamed about doing since my days at Loyola University—no, since my days in high school when I dreamed about being the statistician for the Chicago White Sox. His idea was to put together a volunteer network of scorekeepers to keep score of Major League Baseball games around the country and send them all to a central location where they would be available to anyone and everyone. He called it Project Scoresheet.

My head was spinning. What I could do with all that data! Put it into computer databases. Sort, search, analyze. Understand.

***

You see, I've always been interested in how to use statistical analysis to better enjoy the game of baseball. By the time I read that article in 1984, Bill James had already sectioned off an area in my brain. It's the area where my love of numbers and my love of baseball overlap. That area had already been there in a small way. I'd been playing baseball board games (Baseball Strategy and Strat-O-Matic Baseball) since I was twelve, and I analyzed the numbers seven ways from Sunday. In fact, seven was the key number, as I'll explain.

Here is an example of perhaps the first bit of analysis that I did at a very young age. My favorite player on the White Sox was an out-fielder named Floyd Robinson. I loved him because the announcers told me that hitting .300 was magic, and Robinson was the only guy on the Sox who could do it at the time. In 1961, when I was seven years old, Robinson hit .310 with 11 home runs. In 1962, he hit .312 with 11 home runs. In 1963, he dropped to .283 with 13 home runs. He returned to the .300 level in 1964 with a .301 average and once again hit 11 home runs.

I saw a pattern. When Robinson hit 11 home runs, he batted over .300. If he hit more than 11 home runs, his average dropped. I began to root for Robinson to hit no more than 11 home runs. The next year he hit 14 home runs, and sure enough, his average dropped below .300. And in fact, with his highest home run total, his average dropped to his lowest level, .265.

Batting average was the key. The announcers told me so, and I could see it in the numbers. Until I played Strat-O-Matic (SOM) Baseball, that is. In 1972 I played in a Strat-O-Matic league and drafted players based on batting averages. I got rocked. The manager who had the home run hitters kept winning. His guys would get on with walks, and his home run hitters would knock them all in. That's when I invented my own formula to evaluate players, which I use to this day when I play SOM. It's a form of today's popular OPS formula (**On**-base average **P**lus **S**lugging percentage).

What became clear to me playing SOM was that getting on base was important and so was hitting for power. Batting average still mattered, because—despite the old adage that says "a walk is as good as a hit"—the truth is that a hit is better than a walk. It advances all runners, not just forced runners, and often advances them more than one base. I decided to mix one part batting average, three parts on-base average, and three parts slugging percentage. Divide the whole thing by seven, and you have one number for every player. I used (and still use) this for both hitters and pitchers. And that's why seven is the key number.

***

James caused the revelation in me that I could grow my baseball/numbers brain compartment. I had graduated from Loyola in 1976, and finally in 1982, after six years of intense study and ten exams, I received my Fellowship in the Society of Actuaries. I was exercising the insurance/numbers compartment of my brain. Then a fellow actuary friend, Jeff Schwarze, gave me a copy of the *1982 Baseball Abstract* and said I might enjoy it. For the first time in years I finally had time to read something other than an actuarial textbook. I found myself reading this book cover to cover in every spare moment I had.

A light went on in my head. Here was a guy who was doing with baseball numbers what I had just spent the last six-plus years doing with insurance numbers. I really enjoyed analyzing insurance numbers, but I couldn't believe the same thing could be done with baseball numbers. Sure, the numbers of baseball already existed. In fact, there were already tons of numbers, more than any other sport. A rich tradition of baseball statistics was part of the beauty of baseball. I'd been studying them since I attended my first baseball game

I am a member of a 26-team computer baseball league (The Great American Pastime League) that uses the simulation game Diamond Mind Baseball. Every year we draft major league players and then play a 162-game schedule. We may keep a limited number of our drafted players on our rosters for their entire careers. I attribute much of my success in our league to the theories of Bill James, which I have been using since our founding in 1988, long before they were popularized by *Moneyball*. I use Jamesian principles to evaluate players, set lineups, and develop and employ game strategies. Much of the credit for my successful drafting and evaluation of young players in recent years goes to Bill James' former employee John Sickels.

RICK PHELPS
Investment Banker (retired)
Tucson, Arizona and
Chatham, Massachusetts

in 1963 at the age of eight. James, however, took baseball statistical analysis to a whole new level. He was going deep into the numbers, just as I was doing every day in insurance. But he was finding things in those numbers that no one until him had a clue could possibly be there. I was hooked, and I have been addicted ever since. In fact, Bill James changed the entire trajectory of my life.

In 1983, I walked into the bookstore to get that year's *Abstract*. I was surprised to find it right in the front of the store. In fact, it wasn't simply there on a table, there were copies piled in stacks. Several stacks. Chest high. It obviously wasn't just me who had discovered Bill James.

I bought my copy and read it voraciously. In 1984, it was the same thing. Piles of books. But this year wasn't quite the same for me. I was no longer willing just to read about baseball statistical analysis. I wanted to do it. So when I got to the article on Project Scoresheet near the back of the book, I did my space-staring, walked from the kitchen table, and went straight to the phone. There was an actual phone number in the book to volunteer for the project. I figured I'd get some kind of recording. I dialed the number and a voice answered. Could this be Bill James himself?

It wasn't. But it was Jim Baker, James' assistant at the time. He took down my information and I was suddenly an official baseball statistical scorer! I dove in. Baker put me in contact with Kenneth Miller, the executive director of Project Scoresheet. I told Miller about my background and my love of computers. For example, I shared that I had programmed the entire Strat-O-Matic Baseball board game into my Apple computer and we were using it for my league. Miller realized what this meant: He had a computer geek on his hands. So he turned over the programming of the data-collection software to me. Now I was not only collecting statistics, I was figuring out how to access and use them.

The first season of collecting scoresheets was very difficult, as with any first-time project. The software wasn't ready until halfway through the season. The volunteers worked hard, but the "work" part was getting to a lot of them. After the 1984 season was complete, we realized that there was much more to do. We had all the games on paper, but the computer effort was massive. It became clear to me that to keep this thing going it would require a ton more work, and Miller had let everyone know that he was getting too busy with other projects to stay involved.

Suddenly I realized that I had to step up personally or the entire project would die. I sat down and wrote a huge document to Bill James. I laid out the status of Project Scoresheet and told him how we could still get this thing done. And I volunteered to head up the project. James took me up on my offer.

As of this point, I had two full-time jobs: actuary by day, baseball data collector/programmer by night (and weekends). I did this for two full years. Then, in January of 1987, I took the plunge. I left my actuarial career to try to make it work in baseball. Sue, my wife, also left her full-time job as a computer programmer/analyst to work on baseball statistics as well. We focused all of our time and energy first into Project Scoresheet and then into STATS, Inc. Bill James was one of the investors in STATS, but he was much more than that. Without his help, STATS would never have made it. But it did, because he kept bringing his ideas to STATS, and the rest of us somehow began to make them work.

James still does this with me at my new company, Baseball Info Solutions, in which he is also an investor. Right now, we are cooking up perhaps the most innovative idea he has had yet: We are going to put Bill James online. I don't know what this will look like, but I can promise you that it won't be like anything else on the Internet today.

***

O.K. I'll say it, because I know from personal experience that it is true: Bill James is a genius. As much as I have followed baseball, as much as I have done my own analysis, as much as I have gotten into the numbers, Bill (and I have to call him Bill because he is also now a friend) is always one step ahead—of me and of everybody else. One of the more recent examples was when I was working on my book *The Fielding Bible* about a year ago. I gave him a video comparing Derek Jeter and Adam Everett playing shortstop. Jeter was a Gold Glove shortstop, but all our numbers (and everyone else's numbers) said Everett was the best and Jeter was, in fact, below average. I looked at the video a few times and knew that Everett looked better, but I couldn't pinpoint it. Within one minute, Bill could see it. Everett was playing deeper. He was fielding balls on the outfield grass. Jeter was favoring his weaker throwing arm, having to play more shallow. Jeter was doing a good job on slow rollers, but not making the same, or as many, plays as Everett on other types of balls. Jeter's patented and sensational jump throws were because of a weak arm, not because it was more effective than Everett's plant-your-feet and gun-the-ball throws. Sure, the jump-throws look great, but they are actually less effective most of the time.

I learn from Bill every time I talk to him. But talking to him can be a challenge. Geniuses are often eccentrics, and I'll share one of Bill's eccentricities with you. Don't call him on the telephone. When you meet with Bill in person he is a most charming person. He gives you his undivided attention. He cares about you and your life. He shares his thoughts. But anyone who calls him on the phone is automatically his worst enemy. There have been times when I have just had a great visit with Bill and then called him shortly thereafter. All of a sudden, I had Mr. Hyde on the phone. In the middle of a sentence, he might simply say, "OK, thanks, bye," and hang up. I've learned to avoid the phone with Bill, almost at all cost.

I think I know what it is. Bill is so intensely concentrated on whatever project he is currently working on that the phone is an absolute distraction to him. It takes his mind off what he's doing, and he can't stand it. Bill is always, always, always working on some kind of baseball analysis. Did I say always? There is never a moment when he is idle. So I don't interrupt him. I just wait to see the results of what he's working on.

It is worth the wait.

The Last Word

by Bill James

author of *The Bill James Handbook*
and *The New Historical Baseball Abstract*

You never know what other people know. I remember one time when my daughter Rachel was sixteen, she was in this phase of hating baseball as a way of keeping her father in his place. We were at a game in Texas, and she was reading a book, not paying any attention to the game, and all of a sudden there was this loud booing. "What's that about?" Susie asked me. I didn't know. "John Rocker is coming in," Rachel replied, looking up briefly from her book. We're all in the dark. You never know what information other people are operating on.

One question I get asked a lot in interviews is "Who were your mentors when you were a young man?" I always take this as a sign of how profoundly people misunderstand my career. People like me don't have "mentors"; we have parole officers. I'm joking, but....not really. While I am indebted to many people for what success I have had, most of all to my wife, I was never a nice young man who was being groomed for success in publishing or baseball or anything else. I had a scraggly beard and dirt under the fingernails. I always think of a cartoon that was in the *Saturday Evening Post* when I was a kid....middle-aged couple leaving a movie, woman says to the man,

"That movie wasn't released. It escaped." My career wasn't released; it escaped. I was never supposed to be a famous writer; I was supposed to be a warehouse worker or a cab driver or a truck driver like my brother or a small-town school janitor like my father or, if I worked hard enough, a school principal. In many ways I am more suited for those professions than for the one in which I have worked.

The only thing was, I could never learn to see the baseball world the way everybody else saw it. I am not like a writer except that I write. There was an incident one time in the late seventies when I got a press credential to a Kansas City Royals game against the Mariners....it may have been June 1, 1978. The Mariners gave up, as I recall, ten ground-ball singles through the infield. At the end of the post-game news confab, I asked Jersey Whitehog what seemed like an obvious question: Does this tell us something about the Mariners' infield defense?

This elicited a familiar response....Whitey snorted, and the other writers looked at me like "Who is this tubbledink?" Broke up the news conference.

"It tells us something about their *pitching*," Whitey hollered at us on the way out the door. "They've got a good young infield." I remember Bill Stein was playing third.

As much as I wanted to be a real baseball writer, I couldn't learn to see it their way. I couldn't understand why ten ground balls in a game wandering through the infield *wasn't* a pretty clear sign of substandard infield defense. Whitey—who was an outstanding manager—Whitey and the writers were trapped in an illusion created by the statisticians of Ulysses S. Grant's era. *Pitchers* allow hits; *infielders* make errors. Everybody knows that. That's the way the statisticians set it up at the start of the game; that's the way it was.

They didn't believe in statistical analysis, of course, and so they were in a sense like pacifists who had been taken prisoner by men with guns. Those who are fooled by the statistics are those who are unable or unwilling to analyze them. The illusion of a wall stood between "defense" and "hits allowed". The statisticians of earlier years had created that wall, and baseball men were trapped inside it.

You have probably learned in your life that every form of strength is also a form of weakness, and vice versa. The blind aren't born with exceptional ears; they develop exceptional hearing, because they have to. My career is like that: I have some odd strengths because I have some very unusual weaknesses. I can give you the secret of my success in five words: I don't understand the world. I don't understand anything about it, never have, probably never will. I am sort of like a blind man who builds a kind of theory of what the world might look like, based on the way it sounds. Very often I am mystified by things that seem obvious to everybody else. You watch the sports reporters on Sunday morning, listen to the call-in shows, read the columnists….everybody knows things. These guys know who should be the MVP and who should win the Heisman trophy and who should be in the BCS title games and what is wrong with the BCS system and who is really the number one team in college football and why the Lakers won the NBA or why they didn't and what the commissioner should do about steroids and whether baseball was better in the 1970s than it is now. Man, I don't know any of that stuff. I've been working on that MVP question for thirty years, and I still don't know whether Justin Morneau should have been the MVP or not.

My type of sportswriting is not for everybody. There is a certain advantage in not knowing anything, which is that, since I don't know anything, I am always dealing with questions, rather than answers. I start with the big questions, and I break those down into smaller questions, and then I break the smaller questions down into smaller questions and smaller questions still. Eventually we arrive at the level of factual questions that have answers. In 1975, being unable to understand what somebody was saying about pitching, I started breaking the discussion down until I finally reached the level of asking, "How many double plays were actually turned when Tommy John was on the mound?", and in 1976 I knew the answer to that one, and this type of information is now standard and available to everybody. In 2004, being unable to understand what somebody was saying about this team's offense or that one's, I started breaking the discussion down until I finally reached the point of asking "What exactly *is* a manufactured run? What is it that people mean by the expression, in practical terms?" By 2006 I had an answer to that one, and, in a few years, this will be information that will be routinely available.... You'll be able to go *somewhere* and find out how many runs were manufactured by the 1962 Dodgers, the 1961 Yankees, and the 2003 Florida Marlins.

People are what they are; people today are no smarter than they were in 1700, but they have a hell of a lot more information to work with. Sometimes finding the answers to the little questions gives us an insight into the big questions. There are a lot of things I'll never understand, because the world is billions of times more complicated than my understanding of it. I never understood why John Rocker became a pariah for expressing opinions that roughly 85% of baseball players privately agree with. People now are no less the captives of flawed statistical analysis than they were in 1978, and, now as then, there are statistical analysts who think that their job is to convince people that the illusory walls are immutable boundaries and that statisticians know the answers to all the important questions. But I see the job differently: to admit frankly that we don't understand the problem, and, by doing this, to tear down the walls, and stretch the baseball fan's vision toward the horizon. And to open a few doors for profoundly unathletic people with mismatching socks and dirt under their fingernails.

What success I may have had in helping others to see the world our way....I can't comment. The world changes dramatically every ten years, with or without Bill James. Information is what changes it. I have gotten a lot of credit for changes in the game that I really didn't have much to do with. It's a lot easier to find people who see the world my way now than it was in the 1970s. Virtually everybody now accepts that allowing lots of hits is a sign of bad defense.

Statistics help shape and define the way we see the world. Statisticians have little control over this process. Steve Moyer points out that the usage of Closers would be entirely different than it is if a reliever had to pitch two innings to be credited with a Save. It's a reasonable rule, isn't it? If a starter has to pitch five innings to get a Win, why shouldn't a reliever have to pitch two innings to get a Save?

Did Jerome Holtzman, when he invented the Save, intend to create a game in which people were paid $9 million a year to pitch the ninth inning when the team was one to three runs ahead? Of course not; this change was created not by his idea, but by the interaction of his idea with the forces and the random accidents of history. And the same for me: My ideas have not had any direct impact on the game. Ideas are a part of the mix, like the baking soda in a recipe, like the acid in your stomach, like the resin on the bat. I appreciate your taking the time and making the effort to write and read about me; I appreciate the credit I have so often been given, deserved and undeserved. And I appreciate very greatly the opportunity that the baseball world has given me to be a little part of the mix.

Acknowledgments

First, I have to thank Bill James. When I first asked him if he objected to our doing a book like this, he said he never took a position one way or the other on people writing about him. In fact, he seemed a little bemused about the whole thing. Then, when I asked him to write "The Last Word," he graciously agreed, partly as a favor to me and partly, I think, because he always likes to have the last word.

Second, I have to thank the writers of the twelve main essays in the book. Each one of them responded quickly to the invitation to write about Bill James, and all of them offered insights that only they could provide. They all kept to their deadlines, and they all accepted my editorial suggestions with grace and humor.

Third, I have to thank the "just plain fans" who wrote the sidebars found throughout the book. They all heard about the project in an e-mail we sent out to the customers of ACTA Sports and wanted to contribute to the book. Their comments insured that the book remained grounded in the reality of just how much people in all walks of life appreciate and have been influenced by Bill James.

Fourth, I have to thank John Dewan. He has given me the opportunity to pursue one of my real passions in life: baseball. His is a spirit of generosity and encouragement for so many people, not just at ACTA Publications but also at Baseball Info Solutions, Mission Honduras International, the Dewan Foundation, Camp Dewan, and the many other causes and activities he supports.

Finally, I want to thank baseball itself. It is such a great American game, one that has given pleasure to so many people over so many years. I coached kids' baseball for over ten years; I follow my Cubs every year, even though they always break my heart; and now I have the opportunity to write, edit and publish books about baseball. What more could a guy ask out of life?

Gregory F. Augustine Pierce
Chicago, Illinois
January 2007

Index of Baseball Names

Other Books from ACTA Sports

THE NEW BALLGAME
Understanding Baseball Statistics for the Casual Fan
by Glenn Guzzo
A book for those who are trying to understand what the big deal is about baseball statistics and how these statistics can increase their enjoyment of the game. 176-page paperback, $14.95

THE BILL JAMES HANDBOOK
by Bill James and Baseball Info Solutions
Always the first and certainly the best of the annual baseball statistical analysis books. Contains all the lifetime stats from all the players who played Major League Baseball the previous season. 466-page paperback, $21.95

THE HARDBALL TIMES BASEBALL ANNUAL
Edited by Dave Studenmund
A comprehensive analysis of the entire previous season from the first pitch to the last out, including a review of the playoffs and the World Series. Written by the think tank of baseball writers at the popular website www.hardballtimes.com. 350-page paperback, $19.95

JOHN DEWAN'S FIELDING BIBLE
by John Dewan
The breakthrough analysis of baseball defense that is revolutionizing how people think about fielding statistics. Includes major contributions from Bill James and Baseball Info Solutions. 241-page paperback, $19.95

THE LIFE OF LOU GEHRIG
Told by a Fan
by Sara Kaden Brunsvold
This complete biography looks at the legendary New York Yankee first baseman from the point of view of a fan, revealing what Gehrig and his legacy have meant to her and other baseball fans. 252-page paperback, $14.95

Available from booksellers or call 800-397-2282
www.actasports.com

Other Books from ACTA Sports

BEHIND-THE-SCENES BASEBALL
Real-Life Applications of Statistical Analysis Actually Used by Major League Teams...and Other Stories from the Inside
by Doug Decatur

An insider's look into why, when and how analytical managers and GMs use the practical application of baseball statistics to make key decisions in a game and over a season. Includes the popular "GM IQ Test." 311-page paperback, $14.95

STRAT-O-MATIC FANATICS
The Unlikely Success Story of a Game That Became an American Passion
by Glenn Guzzo

The award-winning book about the creation—and re-creation—of America's most popular sports board game ever. Tells the story of Hal Richman, who beat the odds and invented a game that has been played by thousands of baseball fans for over forty years. 320-page paperback, $14.95

DIAMOND PRESENCE
Twelve Stories of Finding God at the Old Ball Park
edited by Gregory F. Augustine Pierce

A collection of true stories in which the authors relate how they came to feel the presence of God while enjoying the great American pastime as players, coaches, parents, children, or just plain fans. 175-page hardcover, $17.95

THE BALLGAME OF LIFE
Lessons for Parents and Coaches of Young Baseball Players
by David Allen Smith and Joseph Aversa, Jr.
with a Foreword by Peter Gammons

A book for parents and coaches who love baseball and want to be involved in encouraging children to learn and enjoy it. Contains practical advice, true stories about youth baseball, and "Life Skills Learning Drills." 126-page paperback, $9.95

Available from booksellers or call 800-397-2282
www.actasports.com

Advance Praise for
How Bill James Changed Our View of Baseball

As someone who has spent gobs of time thinking about the subject, I devoured *How Bill James Changed Our View of Baseball* the way Bill James goes through a 12-pack of Diet Pepsi. The concept couldn't have been more satisfyingly executed. —**Scott Gray**, author, *The Mind of Bill James: How a Complete Outsider Changed Baseball*

To think of Bill James is to be instantly transported back to your youth, to a time when your mind hadn't yet been clouded, as Stephen Colbert might say, with baseball "truthiness" but was ready to learn baseball's truths. This book is filled with admirers of Bill James, who remember how he helped them fill a void that was prevalent in their lives—baseball or otherwise—to learn something real, something true, and make it a part of them. —**Tom M. Tango**, co-author, *The Book: Playing the Percentages in Baseball*

At the recent winter meetings for Major League Baseball, I saw a general manager carrying around a copy of *The Bill James Handbook*. I'm sure he wasn't the only one. That alone tells me about the influence that Bill James has had on the game. *How Bill James Changed Our View of Baseball* explains why and how this revolution took place. —**Tim Kurkjian**, senior writer and analyst, ESPN the Magazine and ESPN-TV

Writers don't just send their words and ideas into a void. There are real people out there, and a form of conversation is going on even if we only get to hear one side. There's been a conversation going on between Bill James and his readers for over a quarter century. They haven't just listened quietly and moved on—they've been changed. Here's your rare opportunity to hear the other side of that conversation. —**Craig Wright**

If there is one thing that Bill James has demonstrated it is that command of numbers allows an author to use increasingly powerful words. *How Bill James Changed Our View of Baseball* is full of powerful words from writers who know the numbers. Read it and you will learn a lot about clear thinking, fair-mindedness, and the search for truth. —**Glenn Guzzo**, author of *The New Ballgame: Understanding Baseball Statistics for the Casual Fan*